From Behind the Counter

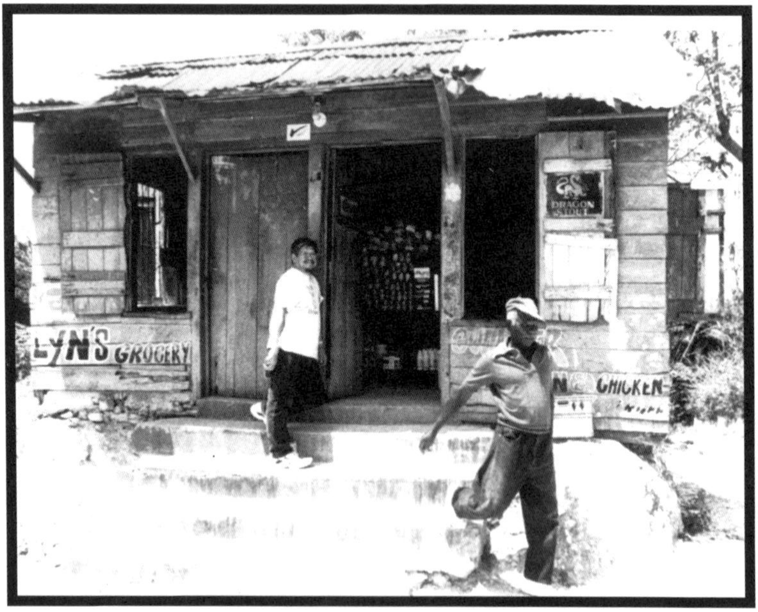
LYN'S GROCERY
CHICKEN

FROM BEHIND THE COUNTER

Poems from a rural Jamaican experience

BY EASTON LEE

Photographs by Owen Minott

IRP IAN RANDLE PUBLISHERS

First published in Jamaica 1998 by
Ian Randle Publishers
206 Old Hope Road, Box 686
Kingston 6

© 1998 Easton Lee

All rights reserved – no part of this publication may be
reproduced, stored in a retrieval system, or transmitted in
any form, or by any means electronic, photocopying,
recording or otherwise without the prior permission of
the authors or publisher.

ISBN 976-8123-49-4 hardcover
ISBN 976-8123-87-7 paperback
A catalogue record for this book is available from the
National Library of Jamaica

Book pre-press production and design by
ProDesign Ltd., Red Gal Ring, Kingston

Set in 10/12pt Adobe Garamond

This is written for our grandchildren:
Daniel, Joelle, Cristina, Kara, Melissa, Stephanie, Kimberly and Rebecca and for everyone everywhere who shares this heritage especially those who have missed direct contact with the "older folks".

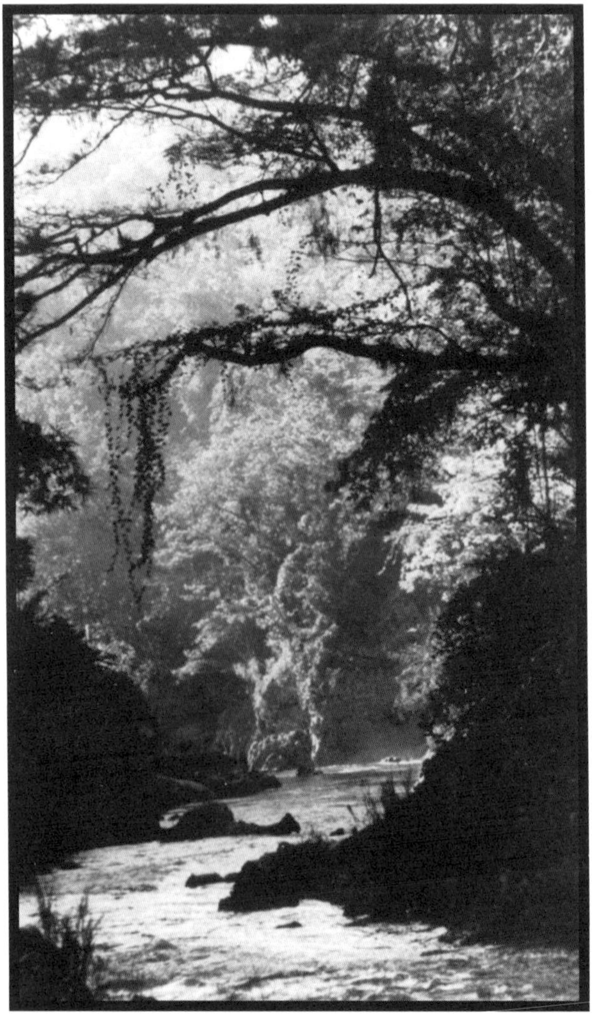

Contents

Preface   *ix*

Acknowledgements   *xii*

Days and Nights   1
    Friday *2* § Saturday *3* § Sunday *5* § Every Day *6* Today *7* §
    Next Day *8* § One Day *9* § Some Days *10* § All Week *11* §
    Every Night *12* § Some Nights *13* § Saturday Nights *14*

My Mother is a People   15
    My Mother is a People *16* § To a Mother Resting *19* §
    Meeme by the Evening Door *22* § Who fa Granny *23* §
    You Will See *25* § Reflections *26* § A Childhood Memory *28* §
    Yes Mama *30* § Woman Praise Song *31* § Woman *32* §
    Mountain Queen *33* § Happy Anniversary *34* §

My Father Inside   37
    At the New Year *38* § The Visit *39* § Best Man *40* §
    Birthday Song *41* § Funnels *42* § Instructions on Equality *43* §
    My Father Inside *45* § Passion's Words *46* §

Church is a Place   48
    My Reason *49* § Holy Thursday Letter *52* § Christmas
    Letter *55* § Prayer at Pentecost *60* § Hymn at Baptism *62* §
    As Fren to Fren *64* § The Rope and the Cross *66* § Dark Valley *69* §
    The Donkey's Complaint *71* § Church and Me *74* § All Prospects
    Please *76* § Pray Hard, Work Harder *78* § Special Prayers *79* §
    Punishment *80* § Day of the Palms *81* § Han go Packi come *83* §
    I Live *85* § Right Church Wrong Pew *86* § Unto Others *87* §
    Forgiveness *88* §

Fun and Games   90
Much "Todo" About Nothing *91* § New Torshan *94* §
Village Joke *98* § Married Story *100* § Gilnock Race Horse *102* §
Married Yes *107* § Wedding Belle *108* §

Serious Things   109
Plain Truth *110* § Day Light Out *111* § Journey *115* §
Word is Wind *116* § Plaiting Song *117* § Message from an
Old Man *118* § Village Tragedy *121* § A Woman's Prayer for
Shelter *123* § Outside Pickney *124* § No Tears for the Wicked *125* §
Pay Day Decision *126* § Mosquitoes *127* § Tracings *128* §
Perception *129* § Strategy *130* § Doesn't it Matter? *132* § Cane
Piece Blues *133* § Advice *135* § Senseless *137* § From the
Sidelines *138* § Getting On *139* §

I saw my land   140
Take A Next Look *141* § The River *143* § Under Banyan
Tree *144* § Consolation *146* § Dark Night *147* §
Corn Time *148* § Drought *151* § The Rain *152* §
Small Eyes *153* § Music Man *154* § Negril Sunset *155* §
Mere Mortals *156* § Santa Cruz – Holy Cross *157* §
In the Park Up-Town, Down-Town *159* § Town Clock *160* §
By The Sun *161* § Introduction *162* § Obeah Dung Deh *163* §

School Days   165
Marbles *166* § Midnight Train *167* § Fight *168* §
Garden Day *169* § Cool Sweetness *170* § Next to Godliness *172* §
Dress To . . . *173* §

Story Time
Story from Death Row *175* § A Sad Story *178* § China Town
Story *179* § Love (Lost) Story *181* § Poor Aunt Margaret *182* §
Aunt B's Days *184* § Nana's Chalk Pipe *187* § Man of the
Morning *189* § Who Stronger *190* § Interference *192* §
Argument *193* § We Is The Best *196* §

Preface

There was a time
when lack of or inadequate communication made it difficult
to reach villages and towns across Jamaica
when news arrived stale for there were few telephones
and no electricity except in the very few major towns
when remote villages saw newspapers days
weeks after publication if at all,
and to have a telegraph office in a village was a great
    achievement
when communities were forced to be self sufficient
when for example people made their own entertainment
playing musical instruments they had made
at dances and concerts at home at school at church
put on without outside help to raise funds for community
    purposes
and people ate well on what they produced, producing what
    they needed,
when caring and sharing was a way of life
when if you had food your neighbour couldn't go hungry
and vice versa 'han go packi come' was how we lived.
Then the old people's word was law
children were seen and not heard and only spoke when
    spoken to
and 'manners' was what you carried all the time
in your school bag your pencil box your pocket in your shop
    basket
or squeezed up between your lunch in your shut pan;
when our people survived some in poverty most with dignity
for they had to lay the foundations for what we reject or enjoy
    today.
The wisdom of the ages was ours gathered from their experience
handed down word-of-mouth to us or by example
in unique and special ways

as they received from grand and greatgrand parents.
The learning came as well from their friends and relatives,
for you were everybody's child.
Nights and days were spent listening as the stories were told
as the songs were sung and the teaching was done
in subtle and not so subtle ways in language and style
rich with colour humour pathos and life robust and haughty.
No chance was lost, no opportunity missed
on every and all occasion the teaching continued
morning noon, good afternoon and night
in home and yard, at school at church (the center of rural life)
in field and garden by river and pond on road and ball ground
on bicycle truck and dray at police station clinic and doctor shop
at market bar and village shop on both sides of the counter
every place all the time non stop.
You learnt how to –
as well as how not to . . .
And who is to tell
but it is that which makes us what we are
helped us come so far
so that now we have worldwide fame for many things
praise and honour, blame and shame alike.
For somewhere along the way
we lost much of that inherited wisdom
much of the pride-giving learning and lore,
perhaps because we looked too much outside ourselves
and our eyes were dazzled by the glitter of other suns
we thought or were led to accept as brighter than our own
and our minds got confused and muddled by foreign things
    and thinking.
Instead of 'making fashion' we followed fashion, blindly
    sometimes.
And after we have tried it all, we yearn now to return to
    the time
when our worth our dignity and respectability
were molded and scolded into our conscious and subconscious
by those who came before
ancestors from ancient lands and civilisations
who met and mingled on this island
starting the creation of a rich and unique culture,
which time will test and prove.

This book, the first in a planned series, joins the many
    existing works
(and there are more to come) attempting to tell their story
and the stories they told, as much as possible in their own voice
giving them a voice once more
trying to recapture even a fraction of that legacy and
    heritage
for the present generation and those to come
so that as we move into the new millenium
they will hear the echo of ancestral voices
even as they hear the voices of contemporary poets
who today sing their story their pain their suffering
their triumph their joy and glory,
in the hope that they will be better equipped to make
    the journey
leaving behind the encumbering baggage collected along
    the way
from those who would have us believe that we are less
    than they
lesser mortals from a lesser source.
Our purpose in our time as it must be in all times
is to help this and future generations realise
that like everybody we are 'somebody'
people of pedigree and worth
all of us.

Acknowledgements

Eternal thanks:
To Mama Lee, Papa Lee, Mama Lowe, Papa Lowe, Aunt Mag, Aunt Gerty, Aunt Jane and Minnie. To Miss Clarice, Miss Vie, Miss Birdie, Miss Zelma, Sta' Sis, Sta' B, Sta' G, Na Na, Mee Mi and Mammie. To Po Po, Ni Ni, Ti Goo, Ah Sow, Shook May, Goong Goong, Ah Shook and Shook Goong. To Uncle C, Uncle D, Uncle Joe, Uncle Jim, Grandpa Hubert Paul Simpson and the host of other persons who were the source of the material. To Hon. Louise Bennett, the pioneer and Hon. Edna Manley (Mardi) for inspiration and courage.

Thanks "muchly":
To Ruth Ho Shing for typing, computing and patience, to Barbara Johnston, Claudell Brown, Suzette Hislop for computer help, to Creative Projects for plenty help and facilities, and to Owen Minott and his wife Margaret for photographs and generosity.

Special thanks:
To Erica Allen, Leonie Forbes, Ruth Ho Shing, Grace McGhie for readings and faith in the work. To Carole Reid, Winston Ewart, Johnny Mack, Grace Jervis and Yvonne Foster, for being loyal fans; to our Church audiences all over Jamaica for their acceptance and warm reception of the readings; To Wayne Chen of Superplus Food Stores, Herman Lee of Magic Whole-sale, J Wray and Nephew, Grace Kennedy & Co. Ltd. and Jamaica Producers Ltd.; Ian Randle and staff for all their help; and to my wife Jean, for encouragement, faith and devotion.

Days and Nights

Friday

Friday afternoon
and half-day school done,
all over the school yard
children play and run
chevvy chase, rounders,
egg and spoon,
flat race and
cricket.
But I must be home
to take my place
behind the counter
through the trap-door,
where weights and measures tables
find ready use
and multiplication and money fraction reign in reality
and each customer
seem more troublesome than the one before
and I grow more bored
by the minute and the hour,
but keep my welcoming smile and manner
all day well into night
for I must not forget
the customer is always right.

Saturday

Marning Miss Clarice
Marning Miss Vie
What a way you looking good
Lawd mam despite everything
by the grace of God
by God's grace we all
survive, a blow fi life.
By the way, you hear say
Claudy lef him wife
You lie
Lef the wife and the seven pickney
and you hear say
Mass Charley bruk him foot again
fall dung offa the horse in the rain
Poor Charley is the third time
And you no hear say
Mother Barnes grand daughter
Bella in the family way
No! What is dat you say?
Yes mam, Simon the big foot bwoy
working with Mister Coley the shoemaker
don't even have cacoon a Asia.
Four pound a flour Miss Carrie
and say him looking woman –
den the other day –
two pound a sugar –
the mother nuh trace me off
Lawd this awful cough.
Yes mam tell me how me tief
half pound a fish and one pound a mackerel –
like say she have anything fi me tek
but me know a what mek
quarter pound a salt pork, penny black pepper –
me dear mam she a try get in pon Boysie
You mean fi you Boysie
Yes mam – the wretch she hot like fire for him
quarter pound a butter
and one pound a fine salt.
Then what a ting dung a post office

see here mam
a never see so much rock stone
fling from all about
a drop on the zinc top
and not a soul know from where.
Shut up you mouth
mussi duppy
me no care what dem say
dat no so-so so.
Four box a matches
two lead pencil –
and me hear say Corporal spen two night
and one day and not even a
puss in sight.
The Post Missis know how it go
for me hear say is not the first time
she know yah, she know.
Lawks look how me forgot the rice
four pound a brown and two pound a white
and pint a cooking oil.
Den you no hear
mad Mavis pickney dem head
take up wid lice
no say me say yah
a di wutliss gal whey di father dey wid
dem ketch it from
and me hear say she
and teacher . . .
hey, hey – see yah
a gone you hear
see you a church
Sunday if life spare.

Sunday

Yes man go church
you madda carry you go
every Sunday . . .
church good thing me know
teach you love God
love mother love father
sister, bredda . . .
love alla somebady . . .
teach
respect old people . . . Yes
church good thing
serve God
but you no stay too long
church over people come home
want cook
want smoke
want drink
want serve.
Good thing serve God
serve customer too.

Every Day

Before cock crow fi daylight
long before morning star drop
see the light in the window
over Fat-man shop
sugar set out
crackers – cocoa-tea
bread and salt butter
cut and wrap from last night
late late.
Salt fish fritters fry from soon soon a morning
ready
for people on the way to grung and work –
hurry can't be late
catch the cool of the morning
and reach before busha lock the factory gate.
One whites dey . . .
gill a pickle salt
big gill a oil
and quarter pound a fish
no badder wrap it
see the enamel dish.
Two bulla cake
two pence hard dough
and penny salt butter.
And no mine the back ache
quattie sugar and penny cocoa.
Every morning same time same place
same ting –
two side a counter.
Like sunrise
like moon shine
like sunset
by the grace.

Today

Yes me buy book
me buy any book you want
clothes and shoes no matter.
Eat good food yes
study you book – dat's better
learning and money – real power.
Too much pretty clothes no good
spree bwoy life that.
Tong Kning know better.
One day you glad.
Today dem laugh.
One day you kick backside
and pay with pocket change
still have plenty money aside –
I tell you no body laugh you
that time you laugh sweet.

Next Day

October country rain
falling since day before yesterday
and everything and everywhere
wetty wetty and cole up cole up . . .
and every tree and leaf and zinc and thatch
weeping cold rain . . .
the bed so warm and you feel sweet
but no late sleeping
work waiting . . . strip off the sheet
feet find the damp way through pants leg
to coarse board slippers strap . . .
wash face –
make haste –
open shop –
watch shop –
lock shop –
sweep shop –
keep shop –
and still the rain falling
like shop-work it can't done
for it start all over again
fore-day morning . . .

One Day

Quarter pound at one and nine
that's five pence farthing
box a matches fi quattie
and one dozen crackers
two pence.
Two pound a mix flour
and gill a coconut oil . . .
full the measure
and give good weight.
Like you no have no sense
pound and a half a rice
bit wut a salt fish . . .
in the enamel dish
hurry up pickney
you gwine meck me late again
and meck me business spwile . . .
see yah me deh pon haste you know.
Mercy him slow eeh
and see it set up fi rain.
Hurry up no roun face chiney bwoy
how much dat come to . . .
come and stop you chat . . .
two shilling and fourpence ha penny
 whey you a say . . .
seet yah . . .
teef so till
two and six
and gimme me right change
ugly squeeze eye bwoy . . .
but Lard the basket can't hole di tings
di flour gwine dash way again
beg you a paper bag no me nice fren . . .

Some Days

You no understan business.
Till full silver yes
paper money look plenty
you think you father rich.
Look see this one shilling
only one ha penny you own
only ha penny profit.
The rest buy goods pay merchant
bring new stock.
But two ha penny make one whole penny
and twelve penny make one shilling
and twenty shilling make one pound
plenty plenty work make one pound
and the clock han go roun and roun
den two den four den eight den ten
soon hundred poun.
Money in till look fat
belong to merchant in town
member that.

All Week

Picnic and garden party
school concert
church concert
cricket match –
you watch only from behind
the counter –
learning to count
without using a finger.
No bird bush
nor wheel
nor race
nor cart
nor swimming in the river
no moonlight walk
only hear your
friends talk
and they laugh
because you 'born and grow'
behind the counter.

Every Night

Smell of pickled fish
mackerel and shad
saltfish and herring
daytime not bad.
But when night comes
make sure you bathe
or you take the smell to bed.
Wash your body
from head to toe
and in between.
With Sunday comes
fresh washed night clothes
for you and the bed
then your nose rejoices
at the smell of clean.

Some Nights

You fall asleep
counting not sheep
but stacks of paper packages
ready-wrapped and packed
along the clean dusted shelf
waiting for tomorrow's
early morning buyers.
One shelf full of penny-sugar
one shelf full of half-pound-sugar
one half shelf full of pound-a-sugar
and crackers rolls
from six to two dozen
with a one dozen in between.
Farthing salt up to one pound
in rows on rows
and when the fine one's done
double newspaper to wrap the coarse –
and it seems like it will never end.
For now you start the flour
and the corn meal
and the pain in your shoulder
growing more real.
Then the voice from the chair with advice
remember wrap the rice
but that's nice, for it's one pound
and two pound bags
to fill two more shelves
before you can see your bed.
No wonder brown paper packages
swim and dance all night around in
your head.

Saturday Nights

Saturday night
shop lock
shelves pack
counter wash down
floor scraped clean of the week's droppings
sugar flour corn meal
made sanitary with washing soda
you feel you could eat off it.
Then my father's generosity opens up
the old ice box to a vast mug of shaved ice
condensed milk
strawberry syrup
thick slices of hard-dough bread
and best butter
at the first bite
we are in seventh heaven
every Saturday night.

My Mother is a People

My mother is a People

My mother is
a mason
a carpenter
a plumber
a painter
a builder.
Our little house
is not fancy but neat
everything works
and there are no leaks.

My mother is
a lick-you-finger cook.
Takes little or nothing
and makes a meal
or bakes a pudding or a cake
that you never taste
the like before or since
except when she bakes again.

My mother is
a dressmaker
a tailor
a shoemaker
a buckle-fixer
a belt-puncher,
behind the old sewing machine
she is a creator of
anything needle and thread can make.

My mother is
a nurse
a doctor
a dispenser
on call twenty four hours a day
seven days a week.
And there is no ailment nor fever
her touch can't soothe,
or the something she brings in

a cup or spoon
won't cure.
And hospital injection
works because
mama rubs it after.
The doctor's medicine works
for she holds your head
and helps you up to sip it.

My mother is
a teacher
a preacher
a lawyer
and a judge.
She's a police officer
a warder
and in good time
the punisher and the executioner.
But you know
you get justice
with love and plenty mercy.

My mother is
a banker
a financial advisor
an investment broker.
Just ask my father
for he doesn't know
how the little money stretches so far
he is only interested that it stretches to the bar.
But mama takes a dollar
makes it two, three, sometimes more
you know she is
a miracle worker
and you wonder how she's not
Minister of Finance
or Prime Minister.

My mother is
a fighter
a tough strong lady
an angel

a gentle soul
with a sweet soft voice
that can take on the roll
of thunder brimstone and fire
if needs be.
My mother is all these people
and many many more.
I tell you
my mother is a people
a whole heap a people.

To a Mother Resting

We learn in retrospect
how we were sheltered for nine months
and emerging
cared for by hands that gently rocked
our early sleep . . .
That washed and cleaned us to
the pleasant baby smell of olive oil and talcum.
Those same hands that smacked your bottom
boxed your ears when you got too fresh,
soothed your brow, wiped your runny nose,
or the streams of tears from your dirty face,
pulled and pushed or gently lead us
into early life and living.
The same hands ordered you to bed,
to homework – house chores . . .
dust the table, feed the fowls, wash the dishes,
cut your nails, clean your shoes, wash your socks,
brush your teeth,
wash your hands you nasty child before you eat.

The same hands that dismissed you . . .
Get away from me you too botheration,
hugged away your cares when you fraid of the dark,
buck your toe or fraid the John Canoe in the park . . .
baked the birthday cake from one egg,
a little flour and sugar,
welcomed and congratulated your triumph of success
or wipe the tears of your disaster even when you big.
Those same hands working late into the long nights
while you growing up sleeping . . .
Hands with no visible tiredness, always turning,
making fashion . . .
with very little or nothing sometimes,
working with needle and thread or the old sewing machine
to stitch up your life.
And when you older, you no wiser,
for you still wonder
how this miracle was possible
to make dinner from a breadfruit, a slice of pumpkin

and one chocho . . .
tomorrow if there is no butter, there's bread . . .
two slices each, sometimes one and a half . . .
and you eat.
You wear not fancy most times, but neat . . .
and clean.
And there's the miracle of the money for books . . .
pen, pencil, music lesson . . .
and school fees and bus fares,
doctor bill, light bill, water rate and taxes . . .
maybe a matinee fare . . .
when the bell ring Sunday morning . . .
bless God, something for the collection plate.

Sometimes bitter disappointment is all the reward,
pain and sorrow the dividend they collect . . .
But pride dignity and self-respect set with you
like a guardian angel for life.
And we know we lucky than most,
for not all have this fortune.
And we grateful . . . and for all the loving . . . we grateful
we give thanks for all that
but most of all that the tender care never cease . . .
No matter what.

For as the Blue Mountains rise
a constant backbone to this island place
so this species of gentle people hold us all together
with the strength of Goliath
mold and shape and pray us
into the image of grace . . . and good
and independence and self-worth
community and nationhood.

And no matter how old you be
or which place you be
you never forget you childhood slumber
cradled in her arms, sung to sleep
with the Alleluia chorus
slumber sweetly my dear,
Jesus loves his little children.

So we charge you . . .
Look upon this noble band of God's chosen . . .
Ordained to the sacred task and
sacrifice of Motherhood . . .
That when next you meet
as you do every day
the mothers who have to be father brother,
uncle and auntie
give thanks and thank the Giver
for the sacrifice is a hard task master . . .
it keeps the eyelids open long, long nights,
swell the feet with long standing,
pain the heart with longer loving . . .
It is a wide river,
A high mountain,
Yet there is rest at last after the tired crossing
and the breathless climbing . . .
to familiar strains of glad hosannas,
redemption coming,
Praise the Lord.
So now to the women who bear children
and plenty who don't bear,
but mother children . . .
we say respect,
more respect.
Give thanks, give thanks.

Meeme by the Evening Door

(for Owen Minott)

I have seen everything.
Happy days and
sad ones too,
laughter and tears,
tasted the honey and the gall
drunk deep from the cool clear waters
of four score years.
Soon, soon now I can rest
these tired weary eyes
this tired weary head
lay down this tired weary frame.
Till then I patiently wait
by the evening door for the call
to hear the Saviour speak my name
giving thanks and praise. Amen.
The old man my lover
still hovering at my neckside
since our youth
and untamed passions made us one.
We made our children and many memories
sharing all, all this time
but he will make his own supper tomorrow
and quietly go to his first lonely bed
perhaps sigh in sorrow
but I'm glad he will have the little great grand
to fetch him water in the red cup
on the window sill.
Come let me bless you
little man-plant
it is time for Meeme to go
but you will grow beloved
love and breed
and nourish
and pass on by.
One day perhaps you forget Meeme
but when the sun set
always you'll remember
every day is a bright new morning.

Who Fa Granny

Wha happen Johnny
Whey di I a say?

Bwoy everything cool
jus leave school
ah just waiting to carry home mi granny
and you waan see is stew peas day today.

You and your granny bwoy –
dat old lady have you saaf.
I cool to you know
yesterday and today too
I skip school
I no fool like you
bus my brain under strain.
Dweet all the time – yeah man –
An you waan see
mi granny don't even know.

Bwoy I know mi granny know
I would never do dat –
so she don't worry,
but you gwaan man
one day you gwine sorry.

Naw sah
I easy – I cool
Hear me now star –
You see mi granny
is as if dem set her pon me,
yeah man
a so all dem ole people stay all di same
just a spwile man business
nag nag nag everyday.
Watch yah, look pon da ole woman deh
di one wid the two scandal bag you see her.
Because a she the traffic haffi stop,
she just a crawl like snail cross di street.
Why dem no jus stay home read dem bible

and say dem psalms
and keep dem self out a harm's way.
Hey ole soul you no see the light change
cross no madda, is wha . . . cho . . .
you no seet, see whey me a tell you
plague man plague in a di busy street. Cho.

Hey bwoy
true you no know
watch you big mout an mine you lose all you teet.
You betta stop you facey chat
you see dat same ole lady you a talk
is mi owna granny dat.

You Will See

I watched my mother
when I was barely ten
toil long hours over many chores.
Try as I might again and again
I could not understand
her eyes getting dark
her hands growing rough
why she laboured so
even in pain.
I ate the food she made
I wore the clothes
I was always in school
there were books pencils pens ink
as if that were not enough
on Sundays the dinner was special
nothing fancy, but plenty, good
and we were in Church singing God's praise.
When I think about all those things
she did what seemed impossible.
When she refused us anything
I couldn't see why
and wanted to know
why, how, when, where.
All she would reply –
You growing, one day you'll see.

In time I grew up
married
had four children of my own.
Now when the calls come
for a host of things,
for food, books, clothes,
school fees, fares, toys,
and nothing seems enough –
I know why my mother's hands
always were so worn, so rough.

Reflections

There's no way
to say thanks enough
for all the years
for all the tears
the care the love she gave.
And when the ages
roll over your heads
times pass
and your beloved lies in the grave
no word of thanks or praise will penetrate the deep
of everlasting sleep
no regrets either.
Your reflection then sharply calls to mind
your own mortality
you know
leaving all behind you must
move to that inevitable place
meet the Father face to face.
My Lord, what will my end be?
My mother told me how it was to start
through the pain of labour
of three long days she prayed –
deliver us Lord.
But in the end her heart
rejoiced at my coming.
There was celebration and great rejoicing
songs and feasting.
Now she's in that place
that he prepared for all.
He told us so Himself
that all who love and serve Him
will be there too.
When I'm called
gladly will I go
knowing that the joy
that greeted me at birthing
will re-echo on that day
with angels' voices
swelled by one who sang to me –

Jesus loves the little children
around the throne of God in Heaven
singing Allelulia, Alleluia – AMEN.

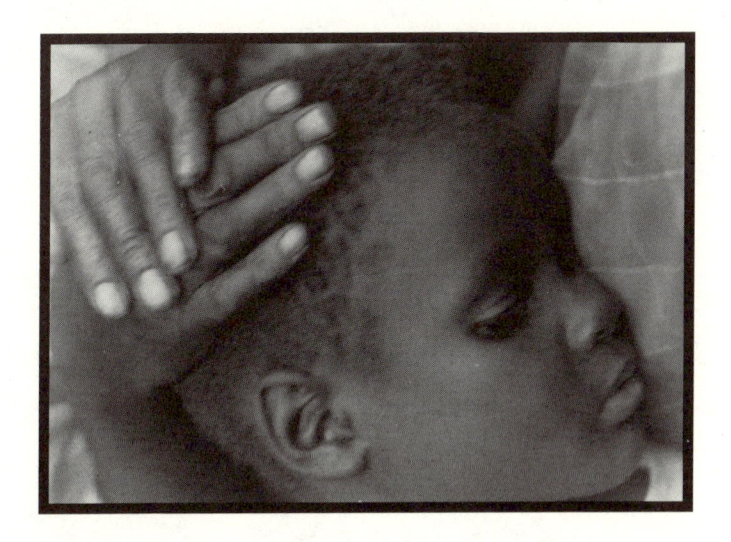

A Childhood Memory

Behind the shop
on the barbecue steps
gathered by my mother
we sing the songs we love
songs we know by heart
melodies of redemption
and the Saviour's love
happy choruses of His promise and His peace,
recite memory gems
and verses from the good Book.
Then nonsense ditties, nursery rhymes,
ones we make up about
people, places, things and times
at school and every which where;
some from our mother's childhood
brought from far off lands
clapping the rhythms, in and out of tune.
Holding hands singing
we watch the full moon
rise in splendour between
the number eleven tree
and the yellow heart breadfruit
over the blossoming corn patch
fall enough on the soft green grass
to light moonshine darling
pass the ball gone round
in and out the window
any such other games and dances
we choose
well into the night
my mother open-throated leading
the playing, dancing, singing
and the gaiety and fun goes on and on
peals of laughter ringing.
No school tomorrow public holiday,
no work either
so father with his friends plays Mah Jong all night
uncle in the kitchen
cooks up a midnight oriental meal

our friends wouldn't miss for anything.
So it is when holidays come round.
But when it's Christmas time,
oh Christmas time
the barbecue is a theatre
friends and neighbours join
to see the nativity live or in shadow
hear the story again in recitation and song
singing the old carols
following a tinsel star
floating precariously overhead
on shoemaker's twine
waxed for strength and ease
leading the shepherds and the kings
robed in the grandeur of old bedspreads
and discarded curtains
to the stool where demurely sits my pretty sister
with the long, black hair
holding last year's doll Jesus-like
loosely wrapped in a drawn thread table cover.
We race to eat the rough toto cakes
brought by my mother's best friend
downed with sorrel and ginger beer
still leaving ample space
for what comes from the kitchen
heralded by the delicious smell.
Father's generosity
opens up bottles of aerated drinks
then we reach to heaven
for there's one whole bottle each.
When finally spent we go drowsily to our beds
first cock crowing
stomachs loaded, mildly aching
heads full of scores of songs
the old old story told and retold re-echoing
we fall asleep knowing
Christmas is the best time of year.

Yes Mama

Yes Mama.
Coming Mama.
Yes Mama?
Yes Mama.
Yes Mama;
No Mama.
No Mama.
Noo Mama.
Noooo Mama.
Wai Mama
Du Mama.
Du Mama
Lord Mama
Du Mama.
Yes Mama.
Yes Mama.
No Mama.
No Mama.
Yes Mama Yes Mama.

Woman Praise Song

Sing the song of woman.
Woman dark
woman fair
woman honey coloured
woman in every shade
Village woman
Town woman
City woman
woman everywhere.

Curly haired woman
wooly haired woman
straight haired woman
woman washing clothes
woman cooking food
woman cleaning house
woman bad, woman good.

Doctor woman
Nurse woman
Teacher woman
woman typing
woman sewing
woman planting
woman rich, woman poor.

Banker woman
Parson woman
Boss woman
Market woman
Politics woman
Sister woman
Mother woman.

Woman in every walk of life
woman in every kind of strife
struggling woman
strong, brave, tender
woman triumphant
woman who is just – woman
Respect, and more respect.

Woman

Woman
mother, daughter, wife, lover
backbone to our endurance
Our hopes . . .
Our joys . . .
Our love . . .
Our sorrows . . .
Our fears . . .

Scarred by time and history
from each dark night
you face the dawn with new resolve.

On your enduring strength we lean
as the land cuddles against the suckling breast
of the blue Blue Mountains
from where the rain comes
the sun comes
life comes.
Woman giving life
sustaining life
and man.

Woman
Jamaican woman
like the blue Blue Mountains
gentle, beautiful, strong,
enduring.

Mountain Queen

Mammie Wint lived on top of the hill, alone
high above the school off the main road.
The pathway winds up up
not dangerous but rough
 through stones and ferns
nice smelling bush, tall mango pimento
orange and tangerine trees,
finally ending at the place where the house appears
set far in at the back of a level common
large enough for a little-boy-size cricket ground
but Mother Wint with machete and hoe many years ago
planted it out with coffee and chocolate
Vincen' yam and cho-cho
gungo, plaintain and banana.
On the mound behind the kitchen
where the fire ash goes
she planted cabbage, calaloo and Indian kale.
Near up to the neat little room and hall dwelling of wattle and daub
white-washed and sparkling in the sun
right close to the line to hang the clothes
there was scotch bonnet pepper, basil, tomatis
and scallion.
In the front croton, june rose, candy stripe lilly
and monkey gun.
At the side of the house
fed by generations of bamboo gutters
stood three large drums filled with water
from the frequent rain
these in turn fed the doona pan set by the kitchen
for convenience.
The place was wide open
except for the barbwire fence
to keep in the ewe and the two kiddies.
Up to this paradise near to the good Lord
where peenie wallie, butterflies and needle case
sport with nightingale chick-man-chick and robin red breast
where the mist hangs low low below white clouds
shading the sun the night and morning stars
the deep blue skies

people trek to buy her produce for they are the best
they come too to pay homage to this lady,
queen of the mountain
of ripe old age,
how much you couldn't tell and dared not ask.
This royal lady comes down once a week only
feet clad in a one-and-sixpence pair of
white crepe sole shoes
to walk the mile and half to the little cut stone church
to meet and greet her Lord and Saviour
chalk pipe tucked in her jaw corner
puffing smoke as she goes
as though that was the fuel
that propelled her strong sure feet.
She is decked out in her customary finery her Sunday best
stiff-starched skirt of old iron blue
topped by a blouse of white cotton cloth
embroidered in lazy daisy by she herself
to match the tie-head framing her time wrinkled ebony face
set with such elegance on grey hair almost white
echoing the regal stance and grace
of people of ancient royal lineage and race.
She walks with head held high proud dignified, bonafide
dispensing good mornings and how-di-dos with majestic air.
In her stride and bearing
the pride of ancient people shows.
Her poor material state
of no account to her royal personage
for who she is, where she's going
from whence she came
she knows.

Happy Anniversary

Is seventy five years now we deh together
married for seventy, today is we anniversary.
No bother ask me why we never married before
dat a no your business, you too fast and inquisitive.
Is plenty plenty things we go through you know
plenty laughter and happiness
nuff grief and nuff tears
nuff nuff eyewater flow
both fi joy and fi sorrow
all these many years.
You see im deh,
ole brute deaf like a rat bat
an miserable can't done,
but ah so im give me trouble
ah so me love im.
Is a long time now we a love
and fine virtue inna we one another.
If me was fi married again
it would have to be him same one, no other
for im is mi husban mi father mi brother
mi very best fren.
Me know some bad minded people
a wonder say
what me see pon him
what him see pon me.

Well every nooko have dem sooko
me an him belongst together
an every hoe have dem stick a bush
an him a fi mi stick
God meck him fi me an me fi him.
An a no really bush me fine him you know,
meet him one day a come from church
love at first sight so dem say
a didn't have to look no furder.
Through ups and downs
prosperity and adversity, thick and thin
whole heap a botheration
we stick together all these years lovin
never think of leavin
never think of divorce or separation.
But lawd
you know how much time ah tink bout murder.

My Father Inside

At the New Year

Clean the halls
sweep the dwellings of the living
and the resting place of the ancestors
cleanse your thoughts of anger, of malice and hatred
as you wash your face in the pure dew of morning
in thanksgiving pay respects to your Gods,
as you pay just debts duly forgiving.
Bring succor to the old – and joy to the children
embrace with love your friends your foes alike
then greet the new dawn
celebrating your dedication and resolve
to make the world a better place.

The Visit

Today my rich uncle
from the city came to visit.

How like my father he looks.
He inspected the shelves
the store room and the business books.
My mother and my sisters he ignored.
A bare murmur of a greeting
was all he spared for them.

I the son and heir
was questioned and advised
on school good manners on business
the Chinese way.

My father looked uneasy and disturbed
till the meal he cooked was eaten
and the whole shop sighed, relieved
when my uncle drove away.

Best Man

When God made man
the first He made from clay
but the kiln was hot, too hot
and God dozed off that day
so that man stayed too long
in the hot oven heat
and missed the mark
his skin came out dark dark.

God made another man
put him in to bake
this time making sure
that he kept well awake.
But in his plight
his anxiety for perfection
he took that man from the oven
much too soon
he came out white white.

So the third time he made a man
he gauged the time
and oven heat just right.
Behold out came the man
perfect balance between burnt black
and pale pale white
colour a warm glowing robust tan.

That day in heaven
so the ancients say
was there great rejoicing
for God had made at last
the perfect man
the yellow Tong Kning.

Birthday Song

My father sang
they say
the day that I was born
the happy songs
his father sang for him
in an ancient distant land.
He sang of sons he longed for
sons to carry his name
strong sons to make him proud.
And my young mother smiled
they say
through the pain of labour
of three long days.
She knew his meaning
though the words were strange
her full heart
beat to the rhythm of his voice
and matched his tune
with the melody of her own fulfillment.
Those ancient songs my father sang
I do not know nor ever again will hear
his voice is long silent to my ears
and my old mother sings no songs
of new-born sons
only now she in silence sits
no more remembering
thinking perhaps
of inevitable partings
glad farewells
and happy sweet reunions.

Funnels

My hands grow
girl-delicate
folding paper funnels
by the hundreds
thousands
tens of thousands.
Day after day
after lunch
after school
before dinner time
before bedtime
before and after
anytime.
Endless paper funnels
each father-inspected for perfection.
I am a funnel machine – the best.
Fore finger in to make the narrow ones for tea
and blackpepper.
Twist once and roll
then pull
wrap over thumb
for red oxide and cocoa
tighter for epsom salts physic
little looser for senna pods and herb tea.
Funnels everywhere
funnels by the millions
for ever and more funnels.

Instructions on Equality

Your ancestors
printed books
a long time ago.
When many other peoples
lived in caves
your forefathers
built palaces
with halls of marble.
Worked in silver
and gold
wove and wore silk
when they ran naked in the bushes.
We carved jade gods
painted fine pictures
cast bronze
made china plate
bamboo and ivory chop sticks
while others ate
with savage
unwashed hands.
We devised systems
for law and order
and for development
still copied to this day.

So tell me now
from where these self-styled betters come?

My son
let no man stir your shame
for the colour of your skin
the shape of your eyes.
You had a name
long before these
walked upright on the land.
Your roots go deep, deep
back to the beginnings of the beginning.
Above all
this you cherish and keep,

no man is your superior
none your inferior
you are better than none
but equal to all.

My Father Inside

Look on my new truck
it has four lights
and a steering wheel
a driver, a battery.
And look –
it can drive by itself.
My father buy it for me
in Miami.
My father buy me plenty pretty things
when he goes to Miami every time.

Is nice
but I prefer my own –
it has a string
and I can pull it
anywhere I want.
I can load it with stone
sand, dirt, anything.
My father made it for me for my birthday.

Cho, is a piece of old board
with four polish pan wheels
it can't even move by itself.
Your father should buy one like mine
that my father buy from America.
My father can buy better than your father
and I don't have to wait for my birthday
for no fool fool old truck.
My father is a buyer man
every day
and he has more money than your father.

My father have a nicer car than your father
My father have a better house than your father
My father taller than your father
My father bigger than your father
My father stronger than your father
My father better looking than your father
My father can beat up your father

My father richer than your father
My father . . . My father inside
where's your father?

Passion's Words

Words spoken in the heat of passion
return again and yet again repeating
to haunt and plague the haughty speaker
in constant and relentless fashion.

Whether of anger or of love
in praise or in condemnation
they find again their own true home
like a wandering homing dove.

And the speaker scarce remembers
what or how intense the speech
while his hearers' expectations
think inferno when they're embers.

So especially to your dear mate
lest you regret the very breath
say no words in passion's heat
but in calm serene collected state.

Church is a Place

My Reason

Say what?
You have a question to ask me!
So what's new?
You always asking some fool fool question or the other –
So what is it this time?
Why I go to church? Well sah!

I go to church to worship God.
Give Him thanks and praise
for all the blessings I receive
pray for my sins and the sins
of those who deceive, tell lie, thief,
and commit all kinds of sin;
for sinners like you and me who in grief
and need God's grace
so one day we can all see
the Holy Face of the Almighty!

Say you want to know
if I can't do that at home?

Of course!
You don't think I do that too?
When I wake in the morning
and see the light
hear the birds sing
pickney cry and laugh
and mi old granny cough
go on bad for her mug a coffee
and cuss mi cousin how him mean...
I give thanks and praise
for life, health, for strength –
If I have pain, I thank Him for that –
If sun shine, praise God –
when it rain, give thanks.
Right through the day at work
or play time,
in the toilet, in the shower, in the kitchen
before tea, before lunch –
I praise the Lord.

On the road, I ask for guidance
and deliverance from bad driving,
moreso from bad-minded people.
I ask Him to hold mi tongue
that I don't sin mi self and swear –
I beg that I don't ignore
the hungry, the poor, the needy –
only the people who ask me stupidness.
At night before I sleep
I praise Him again
I beg for peace and justice at mi home
In England, America, South Africa and Jamaica.
I beg Him to keep me from falling –
for sometimes some people try yu faith
provoke yu peace . . .
The temptation neva seem to cease.
O yes, in my rising, in my lying down
God be praised
Praised be God!

Then if I can do all that
why I bother to go Church?

Because there I meet people
who me and dem think the same thing,
who have prayers to say, hymns of praise to sing
and adoration to bring in
body-and-blood bread-and-wine holy sweet communion
in fellowship and love – one wid the other
together wid the Lord . . .
When I say "The Lord Be With You"
dem say "and wid you"
when I say "praise God"
dem say "Amen"
when dem say "Glory be", I say "Alleluia",
where two or three or more gather in His name
He is present to hallow and to bless!

Say you can't bother
for too much hypocrite and wicked people go to Church?
Well me don't watch dat
dat is between dem and Big Massa.

All I do is pray for dem
and hope dem can pray for me.
When you check it out
more a dem outside the church
than inside you know!
And there is always room for one more.
So meck dem come
for church is not a sanctuary for saints mi dear –
though plenty saint come and go in there –
but a place of refuge for sinners like me
and you tu,
who need forgiveness and the grace of the Father
and of the Son
and of the Holy Ghost,
so all a we find a place in the kingdom.
Sinners like the same ones
you say you know
who go for show . . .
to show off the hair, the clothes,
the car, the jewels, the hat, the boot,
and all such earthly things . . .
who backbite and deceitful,
mean and cubbich and grudgeful,
who commit adultery and fornication,
or jus plain bad-mind.
But God love them tu, like Him love me and you.
And whomsoever will . . .
So the Lord say!
The Kingdom is open to all who seek!

Say what? You going with me next week?
You serious?
There is joy over one who repent in Heaven!
"Alleluia"
What you say?
AMEN.

Holy Thursday Letter

Dear Miss Vie, how you do
and di children and the fambily
and all the rest.
Thank the Lord me hearty tu
mi husban, mi daughter
mi son and mi daughter-in-law.

This is a short note to say
as usual see I send the bun
the toto and some grater cake fi brawta
I hope you feel please
for the price a little bit different
everything so dear, it go up every year
but please don't forget the cheese.

The baking wasn't too bad this time
the old oven behave itself
a get through as usual
but Lord I tired
I don't even know
if I can go church tomorrow.
But all the same I have to go
it would be the first Good Friday I would miss
and I can't make dat happen
Miss Vie mi dear
especially dis year with all the precke
and happenings every which where
Oh yes I will have to be there.

For Easter is a special time for me
from I know myself,
and a dog of my age is no pup,
the season give me time to look
into mi self – see mi self
lift up mi sins to the throne of Grace
to hear the words, Father – forgive them.
Ah Miss Vie
and there is no communion
like Easter Sunday soon a morning

body and blood of our Lord, Amen.
I only hope parson don't put me to sleep you know
for some of the sermon dem so dreary
but me love mi Good Friday service
can't done even doh it long
the reading, the praying and the sermon
di singing of all the old song dem
the meditation on the sorrow and the mourning –
I love it for it give me strength to face tomorrow.
I only hope dem sing all mi favourite hymns
for Good Friday is not Good Friday without
certain hymns and psalms as you well know –
Jesus my Lord is Crucified, Old Rugged Cross,
Were you there when they Crucified my Lord,
When I Survey the Wondrous Cross
Ahaii!!

I only hope the organ don't play too fast and loud
for dose hymn must sing in a slow and
compounded way.

I hope we get the usual crowd –
you ever notice Miss Vie
don't care how church empty the rest of the time
how it well full when it come to Good Friday
and Easter Sunday
and parson glad bag out to burse
plenty collection full up the purse.

What a life
but him have to live tu,
me carrying a nice bun for him.
Me know im wife bake
but she can't bake like me.

Don't worry if you get hungry
I carrying your own tu
so you don't forget the cheese.
I should close now for I have to go
fry the fish and bake the bammy
one million other things to do.

By the way me get me new dress
a nice purple one, Miss Vie –
for me little tired of the black
and a nice black-and-white hat.
Only thing, I have to wear white shoes
as the black one pinch me – is a little tight –
but don't the white will look alright?

And me get the Easter dress already tu – white –
me big son wife, me daughter-in-law
the one who is the teacher
she send it for me – nice so till
and a lovely white hat to go with it
with a pink rose in the front, lawks
me really love dat.

Yes man, Easter going to be gran,
the choir a practice the anthem
we sounding good an strong.
I am arranging some good food and drinks
for after-service snack when we come back
from church.
So mi dear Miss Vie – I have to go
can't stay long
I would write a long letter
but see with me I have plenty to do
walk good and take care of yourself
and say your prayers till we meet
in these times you have to be
always on your knees,
God bless you Miss Vie
As always, your friend Burdie.

P.S. Don't forget the cheese.

Christmas Letter

Dear Miss Vie,
Just a short note to say howdi do.
We is all well, husban, pickney, the gran one dem
and hope you hearty too.
Give thanks.

What a way the Chrismus creep up pon we so sudden.
Well mam . . .
Independence no dun good yet
baps – Chrismus breeze start blow
nice though,
and braps Chrismus deh pon we.
An the bitter bush,
the yellow Chrismus rose dandelion,
and the wild daisy all bloom out.
Jamaican Chrismus yellow and pretty fe true
pity Chrismus come but once a year.

Well see I sen the sorrel,
some gungo fi di rice and peas,
and white yam fi roast,
me know yuh husban love dat.
Mi dear Miss Vie,
what a way things dear,
but a so it was last year
and the year before that year.
Is a good thing me plant my own.
Me naw boast
the artritis a kill me but me have to try Miss Vie,
me no complain – me no worry,
me use what me have and satisfy.
What me can't afford, me do widout –
give thanks – no laugh –
what me have, haffi do.
Whey it mawga, a dey it pop off mi dear,
an Chrismus comes but once a year.

Den how di bakin go
I hope the cake dem come out nice –

you always bake the nicest cake.
I never forget last year – what sweet so?
And I sure I getting the usual.
Tomorrow is gran market day
I can't write a long letter
much as I would love to.
There is the load to pack.
I have nuff tings to sell,
the yam bear so tell
the gungo plenty
and the sorrel in good quantity.
And Miss Vie, a have fourteen of the best cock chicken –
dem no start crow yet –
an weigh nearly six pounds a piece.
I sure I will get a good price
for people prefer dem to pullet mi dear,
dem say cock meat swell –
I don't know bout dat
but give thanks – give thanks
for Chrismus come but once a year.

An see here Miss Vie,
you should see the skellion, tyme,
the carrot and tomatis
Aunt Sissy have –
pretty like money.
I hope she set the right price
and no bodder sell it fi dubloon a joint
like how is Chrismus
for you know how she greedy –
It not right –
me meck mi conscience be mi guide.
Listen nuh Miss Vie,
I hope you coming to church
for Chrismus watch night service.
Parson sey some outside people
coming to sing fi we.
I hope dem sing sweet
for me love the carols dem
especially when dem sing dem
with alto and bass –
you know what a mean.

I hope dem sing my favourite . . .
"Once in David's Royal City".
The children practising up the manger scene
and things so busy – so confusing
everybody have no time to spare –
Is a good thing
Chrismus comes but once a year.

Stop for some chocolate tea
and hard dough bread when yuh passing.
Come soon, so we go early an get a good seat
near the window as usual to get the breeze.
For when I hear the music
feel that breeze blow
an a close mi eye
I think is heaven I reach
the only disturbance is if parson
preach too long.
But is something I live for the whole year roun
I love it can't done,
Pity Chrismus comes but once a year.

Well Miss Vie,
I really apologize for this short letter,
next time I will do better.
But see wid me
I have to try and get a little sleep
for when you come from gran market
ef the truck no bruck dung
you just have enough time fi tidy
and get to church.
Is a rough time, but me love it,
since me was a chile.

You remember when we was little Miss Vie,
how we use to enjoy the season –
new clothes, new shoes,
fee fee balloon, Chrismus toys and hat,
fire racket, John Cunno
and concert galore
and much more besiden dat.
The food was something else

we never know the reason
but that was the only season
you eat as much as you like –
you parents beg you to eat,
food and sweety can't done,
and you get a whole bottle
of aerated water fi you one.
Not to mention the colic
and the castor oil after,
Is a good thing Chrismus comes only once a year.

But you know Miss Vie,
the best part is the part
some people leave out.
How Jesus born to a poor country woman like we,
how so many people adore him in the manger,
how up to now we still worship him.
For him come to bring peace
and justice and love.
Peace on earth and goodwill to all men,
an woman tu – everybody.
If only we all remember dat Miss Vie –
what a way this place woulda nice –
what a way we would live good an happy.
But human nature funny,
we only see things and money.
For money we even sell Christ,
Ai mam.

But me pray every day
not to forget him goodness an him love.
Me no worry or fret
for the same baby born Chrismus time
is the same one come dead and rise again
to save we soul and bring salvation.
The same little baby
The Saviour of the world – Amen.

Walk good yah Miss Vie
till I see you.
Sorry the letter so short,
but see wid me mi dear –

so much to do
time so busy
so confusing –
good thing Chrismus only come once a year.

Prayer at Pentecost

Hear the rushing wind
the rushing mighty wind
that blows the fire
from the four corners of the highest heaven
the mighty breath of the Almighty God
Amen.

Come Holy Fire
Oh Holy Fire come to me
burn His seal upon my heart and tongue.
Today oh God
give me utterance
to speak thy power and thy name
the revelation
of your awful truth and fame
Alleluia.
Oh mighty God, everlasting God
set us all alight with the heavenly flame
and all who speak
the message of your Glory.

Life giver
Power giver
give the power
that all mankind
in every native tongue
will hear the sound of your great voice
speak the word
thundering in every ear
Amen. Alleluia.

Holy God of Pentecost
come now and join our cloven tongues
in sweetest unity
that here on earth
though now in many different ways
each native to his own time and place
in traditions of each separate race
we speak with one voice

and that thine own
Amen . . .
One truth uphold and that thine own
Amen . . .
Confess one name and that thine own
Almighty and eternal God
Amen . . .
Alleluia and for ever
Amen . . .

Hymn at Baptism

Over me, over me
let the cleansing waters flow over
roll over me
over my yielding body
temple of my soul.
Let it flow now
no longer dare I wait
come now my brother
to your duty by the sweet shimmering
cleansing river – healing stream.
Plunge me now beneath the flood
to start the journey home.
Do not say you are unworthy
for the Father gave that task to you
as He gives to each and all
so I, even I
His truly begotten son
begotten before all worlds
must now obey
the Father's will and full command.
So let it be – let it be now
now the healing time
time of righteousness
time to purify.
Oh let the cleansing waters flow over,
let it roll over me
over my yielding body
temple of my soul.
Holy messenger
Dove of heaven
Alight upon my head
bring the blessing
from God's right hand.
Now take my hands my cousin
my brother and my friend
and help me through
this solemn transformation.
Now, now
speak the words He gave to us

and open up the way
the way to all salvation.
In the name of God the Father Almighty
come I the Son
and here receive the Holy Spirit
now for ever three in one and one in three
God the Father
God the Son
God the Holy Spirit
Blessed Trinity
Amen, Amen.

As Fren to Fren

God, good God,
you old sneak
what this you doing to me?
Things going so well
I don't feel so weak.
The pain in mi shoulder
not too bad now
since I rub it
with the Tiger Balm last week.
I was just saying to mi self
mi old fren answering mi prayers
the house leak fix
the water tank full
the two yew give me six kiddy
and the old cow drop a pretty heifer calf.
The breadfruit bear, plenty pear
I making a few dollars
from the neeseberry and the ackee
and I can smile sometimes laugh.
Jus when I open mi mouth
to tell you thanks
praise your name again
all of a sudden
no warning, no shame
you old brute you drop this pon me – Ahi!
How I going to manage?
Lord sometime you hard you know.
Sometime you treat me like a outside pickney.
I not really complaining
but though I know you goodness plenty other times
sometimes is as if you forget I old and tired.
I know you don't sleep
but sometime you doze off – no true?
So a talking to you as fren to fren
is only fair you know
since you give me the load
you obliged to give me the strength
and to clear the road.
Don't get vex wid me

you know I will do what you say
go to any length
morning, noon or night, any day
only – give me strength, hole mi han,
remember say is me one
for you take him away
ten years now, and tings rough.
God you see and know I tired
and I long to see you so tell
so meck dis be the last time
you put me through this hell
an treat me so rough
you hear mi ole fren?

Alright? Alright. Amen.

The Rope and the Cross

Suspended on the timeless cross
of all our mortal shame
twixt earth and sky
twixt life and death
the God-man in His glory
in sacrifice supreme,
by kiss betrayed, for filthy silver
given and repaid,
fulfilling that for which He came,
that which His God ordained,
with His last breath
forgiveness breathes for all Mankind.

And she who gave him life in mortal flesh
approach the cross with halting steps
and burning breast
rejoicing in the meaning of His passion and His love,
reliving now the promise
made at mid-morning of her maidenhood.
Her limbs and frame so describe her joy and her pain
the sorrow and the gladness mingled.
For this He was born
for this I bore Him,
Alleluia . . . Alleluia
Glory Alleluia.
And yet another in the shadow of the cross
now views the rope that stilled the life she made.
With stance distorted by anguish and despair
questions from shrivelled womb
echoing in vile contraction . . .
Is this for which my purity I yielded?
Is this for which He came?
My son, my son, my only son.
My son, my son, my shame.

Once maidens mild
now women grown
to sorrow and to gladness.
The one rejoices sees the thorny crown

the Royal diadem soon to be
the drops of blood
this human god now bleeds
the jewels that His robe of kingly purple will adorn
when He shall come with greater glory
in His father's kingdom.
The Other seeks the flaxen twist
coiled in nooselike taut finality
and begs the same embrace her throat and neck
to still the howling voice of her great shame,
oh woe . . . oh woe . . . oh woe . . .
eternity damns his name.

Each now the babe she bore remembers
the child that played in warm noon sun
beside the evening door,
the man each came to be
and that their cross-ed paths
should lead to man's own destiny.
Thank God
praises and glory to our God she sings
my Son, my Lord, my King alleluia . . .
My Son, my God, my Saviour, Glory Alleluia.
And even through her glad rejoicing,
she hears the echo
in a sorrowing mother's bosom,
My God, my God, my son, my shame,
my fatherless, friendless, lifeless son.
My God, My God,
has thou forsaken me in my eternal blame?

And so two mothers' prayers
as perfumed incense rise
to heaven in solemn intercession
for mothers now and yet to be
through all ages,
and so to all eternity.
Oh God Creator,
forsake us not in this our travail
whose frail vessels here we are
set for thy purpose and thy will.
Teach us to bear our womb fruit

the twofold pangs of pain and joy to endure,
that bittersweet draught that we must take
that motherhood so bestows.
Amen . . . Amen . . .
Glory Alleluia . . .
Alleluia
Amen.

Dark Valley

In my darkest hour
I try to forget the pain
my eyes close
my mind goes to the place
where once your loving hands
soothed my brow
I cling to your hem
a little child again.

Still holding on to your vanishing shadow
I dare not open my eyes
the agony and the noon day sun
have shattered my dreams
blotted the skies.
My mind keeps your pale scarf
in vain to preserve your lingering memories.
For the stream of life is unfeeling
so dreadfully unfeeling, unrelenting.
Even though I revive the memory over and over
it too I know will vanish
fade away in the dark valley
where now in the shadow I must walk.

To you I ran crying
my mother
my finger pricked
my knee bruised and bleeding
now a thorn-wreath wrapped around my head
speaks my purpose and my lot.

Nails tear my flesh
cold steel breaks my side
releases the crimson tide.
Engulfed in agony
I must go now
make the journey set
and yet
comforted by the knowing
I return again to you.

So with your tears
in the hallowed name
bless my journey now
but a little while the pain is gone.
We rise anew to life everlasting
never to die again.

The Donkeys Complaint

All of you
high and mighty
who look down you noses
on other people
you consider inferior
for whatever reason,
man or woman
who you decide is
not as good as yourself
who you call degrading names
and bad-talk and back-bite
who you low-rate,
because of how they dress
how they look
how they talk
how them skin stay
how them eye stay;
just listen to me
for when donkey bray
is not just noise,
we have reason.
Take for instance
you call me jackass
not so much to identify,
but to down-grade me
to make out
that I don't have any sense
the lowest form of animal –
same way you treat people,
and now-a-days
in woman freedom time
you call my sister
jinnyass.

Anytime somebody
don't understand you
or you don't understand them,
is never your fault,
you call them ole jackass.

Sometime you shorten it
to plain ass,
and nobody escapes.
The teacher is a jackass
the minister is a jackass
the doctor is a jackass
the M.P. is a jackass
I even hear people say
that the Parson
is a jackass,
and the commissioner,
the bishop, the barber,
the waiter, the hair dresser
the bus conductor same ting,
just because you disagree
with what they do, or say.

I hear you all say
every jackass think
him pickney is a race horse.
So what's wrong with that?
When you come to it
race horse,
cow, goat, sheep,
dog, puss, mus mus
nightingale, pattoo
and john crow –
earthworm, lizard and ants
God made all of them
every living one,
including me and you.

When story really come to bump,
don't ever forget
is we same one
carry the hamper a provision
you great granny sell
to put plenty of you through school
and furnish you education.
So now you, you father
and you pickney dem,
you whole generation

is big shot
in big position.

And remember say
that it was a lowly jackass
who carry the Virgin Mother
safely to Bethlehem.
And it was another donkey
like this said jackass
who carry the Master
into the holy city Jerusalem.

He didn't choose a thoroughbred
that race at a popular track
nor an imported stallion
or camel,
or a chariot.
It was on the back
of a lowly jackass
he chose to ride.
Remember that
and humble yourself
get rid of your pride.

So next time you feel
you better than me
or any other animal
human or otherwise,
remember
I trod on the palms they waved,
the robes they spread
on the dusty road
and cantered to the chant
of Hosannahs
loud and lusty
carrying the divine and sacred load.
For twice on my back
rode the Prince of peace
the Son of the living God.

Church and Me

My mother held my hand
and lead me gently to the church
I was no more than three
but I remember well.
All through the services
I slept leaning on her shoulder
munched the biscuits she carried in her purse.
Church didn't mean a thing
but I learned to sing
Jesus loves the little children
and if he loved me, I liked him.

Suddenly I was ten
and just didn't want to go again
so every Sunday I had more aches and pains
than you will ever know
belly ache, tooth ache, ear ache,
every part of my body ached
funny they all disappeared when it was too late to go.
That didn't impress my mother,
after a while my father's old leather belt
or the tamarind switch she cured
for such occasions
took up the case.
If that was not enough
she grabbed my hand,
and pulled and hauled
no matter how I bawled
she was stubborn, she was strong,
before you could say "fe" I was in Sunday School
with all things bright and beautiful,
all creatures small and great
watched by my mother with the tamarind switch
standing guard outside the gate.

Then I was sixteen
church was lovely
because of all my friends
church was where we met

we questioned everything the smart set
would do anything
afraid of nothing
except, my mother's upraised hand
ready to box some sense into your head
if you get any weird ideas.
Church was for us a meeting place
to socialise and profile
but all the while she did not make you forget,
a sacred place of worship
where you must in reverence be
so one day you could see God's face.

I was a young man now
had other things to do
mine was the choice
I could do what I pleased
I stayed away
except for funerals and weddings
I was smart –
church was such a bore.
I didn't enter the door for a long long time
and that broke my dear mother's heart.

She prayed hard and long I know
while I went merrily on my way
until one day I can't explain how,
I heard no voices, saw no light,
must be God himself
who brought me to his house once more.

I found myself in my accustomed place
a little child again
there to fill my own needs
to fill the vast empty space
the aching void.
I learned again the old familiar song,
the old familiar prayer
felt the peace God alone can give.
Now I thank him daily
that my mother was so stubborn and so strong.

All Prospects Please

The rock is solid
forming the mountainside
from time before time
when God stretched his right hand
and his left hand
moulded the hills, shaped the valleys
fashioned the earth.

The waters he ordered
placing them in convenient spots
filled with fish, shrimp, crab, oyster and conch
water lilies and bull rushes and water weeds.
He sowed the seeds, he planted the trees
great mahogany, oak, pine, cedar,
cassia, guango, mahoe, and plenty more beside
and climbing in and out, all manner of vines.

Below on the fertile earth he placed the grass
the delicate fern, shame-old-lady macca
wild daises, forget me not, black-eyed Susan
roses, dandelion, sorrel and susumba.
Breadfruit, yam, cassava, banana,
apple, plantain, cashew
and all manner of other trees
bearing food for man –

Oh yes; man.
He made man from clay
woman too, they say from his ribs.
And everything pleased God,
sun, moon, lightning, thunder, rain
fish and birds, wild beasts
tame beasts, jackass, horse, hog
cow, mule, mongoose, snake and dog
butterfly, gingyfly, mosquitoes and fleas
cock roach, lizard, galla wasp, toad and frog
lion, tiger, elephant, goat.

Everything, every animal, every plant
great and small

all, all pleased the creator except man –
only man, human – only man is vile
man alone displeases man alone causes God pain.
Think about that for a while even just a little while.
To the only creation that gives God grief
God gave Jesus Christ his only son.

Pray Hard, Work harder

I am really sorry
I didn't come to prayer meeting yesterday
and the day before.
I know you all
was praying hard for
help to assist
with the building of the watertank.

But while unno was praying,
mark you praying is very helpful I will admit,
I was carrying
two jackass load of stone from down the gully
so the foundation could start
soon as the mason
ready to begin the work.
For no matter how hard you pray you know
we still need to start the building.
God help those who help themselves
and me believe into that.
So while unno a pray
me wi carry one one
load of stone,
and as me journey
so me sing praises to the heavenly King.
Me work meanwhile me pray
for it can't happen by praying alone,
as mi granny use to tell me
faith without work
the Bible say
no put pot pon fire.
So while you pray hard
you must work twice as hard.
Yes man!!
For some time you know
the Lord need a helping han.

Special Prayers

At Sunrise
With each sunrise Lord my God
again your holy name I praise.
Father son and holy spirit,
blessed to the end of days.
Take my thoughts, my words and deeds
and match them to your sacred will,
bless me this day with all my needs
and with your grace my whole life fill.

At Sunset
As I lay down to sleep tonight
your praise will neither wane nor cease
guard and shield me saviour friend
grant me rest and perfect peace.
Keep me safe till morning comes
when refreshed I rise to tell your story
to do whatever you command
and sing again your praise and glory.

At Eucharist
Forgive me Blessed Lord all my errors and my sins.
Open my heart as I my mouth
to receive your precious body and your blood.
Dwell in my body and my soul,
make me pure, within, without.
Keep me worthy, keep me holy,
for ever and for evermore.

At the End
When my end on earth draws near
and sleep everlasting creeps around my weary head,
shield me then from pain and fear
as through the shadowed valley I must tread,
then lead me safely to your side,
there for ever in your eternal light
to live and sing your power and your glory
Holy, Holy, Holy, God of power, God of might
Holy, Holy, Holy, God of power, God of might, Amen.

Punishment

You see you
how you so wicked and bad?
What make you do that?
You know is a sin?
You know is badness?
God gwine punish you
God gwine make you suffer
you bad little brute.

Move from me before a kill you
wid beating tonight
and take whey the
new boot your mother send.
On top of that
you so bright
come tell me lie dry dry so
like puss bruck coconut eena you eye.
Satan gwine teck you whey.
As a matter of fact
you know what is true
if you know what good fi you
fine yourself over pastor today today
an confess you sin you little devil
and when you done,
pray an ask God pardon
for your wickedness.
Craven, long belly brat
you gwine burn in hell fire.
Eat out you father crackers
and come come tell me say is rat.

Day of the Psalms

What is that sound, I wonder?
Look through the window
coming way down the narrow road
such a crowd
what a sound
men, women
girls, boys
shouting, singing
and who is that on the little donkey
feet nearly touching the ground,
not even a saddle
or a piece of rag?
Just like we used to ride
when we were boys? bare back
such a nice face, calm, serene
but what a mob,
palm branches waving and flowers along the way.
What is it this day?
Never heard so much shouting
seen so much dancing in the road
and the little donkey
frightened and burdened by the load.
Do you hear what they are saying?
Hosanna!
Hosanna? But why Hosanna? Why the blessing?
They come nearer
the shouting grows louder
and louder
Hosanna! Hosanna!
Hosanna to the Son of David!
Blessed, blessed is He
who comes in the Name of the Lord!
What is this?
This acclamation?
This adulation?
And he sitting on the donkey
seems unconcerned
as if He isn't hearing.
They are hailing Him King –

King of the Jews,
Messiah.
He is right below us now
he looks up at me
as if He doesn't understand,
bewildered it seems –
But those eyes compelling
that noise
that shouting.
It's the carpenter of Nazareth!
Him they call Jesus, Master, Teacher
they say He has come to rule over Israel,
but He seems unimpressed.
Perhaps He knows too well
the voices that today with praises swell
will return tomorrow to
shout His condemnation
when all the Hosannas
give way to evil shouts
of death and yet
He rides into this sad city
propelled by the force of His destiny
no mortal man can hinder,
to suffer to die
for sinners, offenders all
for pardon and salvation
to save the whole world.
Oh save me, unworthy and unrepentant.
Ride on!
Ride on, King Jesus,
Ride on.

Han Go Packi Come

The Good Book say
show kindness to one another
help you brother and you sister in distress
God for that will bless you abundantly.
Old time people say
han go packi come
as you measure to your neighbour
it will measure back to you.
So all dem mean cubbich people
can stay there expecting bounty
when dem hoarding up everything
for dem self.
You must help the needy
and don't be so greedy.
Remember –
cast you bread upon the waters
you will find it after many days.
So you give –
so you get.
Sometime the bread no come back just so.
Sometime you wait long
if you not strong
you give up, lose you faith.
Not mi granny
for, sometime, she say
you no get back bread –
you get crackers
you get biscuit
sometime you get bun, and cheese
sometime you get back pure breeze
sometime you get cake
with icenin pon di top
straight out of the master baker shop.
And you wonder and you ponder
what you do to deserve that blessing.
So me don't fret me don't bet
me no get angry
me know say the Good Lord provide.
As long as me have bread

mi neighbour can't go hungry
if me have fire – you have peas –
we can cook
some fi you – some fi me
ascording to the Good Book.
Yes mi dear – me will always share.
for me love cake wid icenin you see.

I Live

(for Edna Manley)

        Four days dead
        entombed
        His sisters weeping
        wish their Lord was near,
        He loved the dead man so
        even so all flesh perish.
        Weeping too
        He speaks of resurrection
        and life eternal.
        Misunderstood he stood by the encasing rock
        and loudly called his friend by name.
        Forth came he alive
        forever free.
        Lord you know me
        You called my name
        now I die no more
        but safely rest in your eternal care
        My Lord my God
        I believe, I believe.

Right Church, Wrong Pew

Inna dat same church
jackass years ago
when mi granny use to carry me
a Sunday-day time
things wasn't like now-a-days
when pickney an any somebody
can siddung any where dem choose.
In a dem ole time days dey
people use tu have dem special bench
with dem name pon it
an you couldn't siddung eena certain seat.
Yes me know you have the place where you like to sit
but ef you come late and your seat occupy
you cut you eye and fine another one
an no bodder gwan like say you own it.
Ah no dat me mean.
You see if you siddung eena one a dem seat whey mark,
or whey everybody accept say a special people seat
dem raise drawers you know
as if the Lord really watch dat
which part you siddung
or whether you mawga or you fat, high or low
When me did little it use to burn me so till
sometime two front bench empty empty
a wait pon Busha an im family
even when church full up
and dem put wi fi siddung pon altar step
an plenty time dem no come.
Me glad dat done wid yah,
and whom so ever will
can siddung whey dem want.
An ef me inna you seat no badder mel me
for the Lord see we all no matter whey you deh
back or front, bench middle or bench en
and if you wan siddung siden you fren
memba a eena di Lord house you deh
just ask me nicely me will oblige and move
it not necessary to gwan
like you have something fi prove.

Unto Others

You hear what the scripture say?
You must be kind to one another,
and do good to each other.
If you can't say good
shut your mouth
an don't say bad neither.
You know finger never say look yah
it always say look deh
but when you point one finger pon somebody
four a point back pon you.
If you plant peas
is peas you going to get
if you plant corn
don't expect gungo
as you sow you reap
so live so you have no regret,
don't put gravel inna nobody shoes
for you will fine macka or tack inna fi you.

Forgiveness

Walk good
and the good Lord go wid yu
you and yu children
yu children's children
unto the third and fourth generation.
It teck me a long time to come to this point
where a can put aside the anger an vexation
an I can say dat an mean it from me heart
after all yu do me
after all di wickedness
me who never trouble yu yet
me who never even say yu eye red.
But walk good Miss Carro
though malice an enmity is yu trade
teck mi foolish advice
put dung inniquity
or yu wi walk an beg
for obeahman money never dun pay.
Yu walk all about all di while
interfaasing in everybody business
causing more worries dan John read bout
yu spen yu time
a fan fly offa other people cow head
while your own leave to spwile
but mine dem gi yu big foot
or tun you mout backa yu
mine when yu tink is peace an safety
is sudden destruction reach yu
but dat won't be my doing mi dear
me don't deal inna dem tings.
God see an know
I forgive yu as a hope an pray for forgiveness.
Walk good
Miss Carro
walk good
an teck heed
put dung evil
an seek salvation
and pray daily

dat the wrath of God don't descend pon yu
but dat Him will bless yu
an prosper yu
even to yu third and fourth generation
an beyond dat tu.
So walk good Carro
walk good
and di good Lord walk wid yu.

Fun and Games

Much "To Do" About Nothing

Whoi mi eye, mi eye
whoi – whoi
Percy what happen?
Ohi – ohi – mi eye, mi eye.
What do you? What's wrong bwoy?
Joe lick out mi eye mama
Joe lick out mi eye.
Ohi – ohi – ohi . . .
Say what?
Come here meck a seet.
Lawd have mercy, look how it bleeding
the eye must blind.
A who you say dweet?
Ohi – ohi – a Joe mama, a Joe.
Who you say? Miss Eva ugly bwoy
wid him head fava Appleton tractor.
Call him faada
and one a you run go call nurse.
Lawd mi God, look how the blood a flow
the eye must blind, the eye ball burse.
Ohi – ohi – mi eye, mi eye.
Whai – whai – him eye blind.
Whai ohi – whai ohi –
Worries never cease
mi one bwoy pickney lose him eye.
Call teacher, call parson, call police.
Whai – whai – whoi – whoi
whai – ohi –
Nurse a glad you come mam
a glad so tell.
Miss Eva ugly bwoy Joe
lick out Percy eye and blind him mam.
Ohi – ohi – ohi.
You wait till a ketch him
a gallows fi me, me a tell you
a heng dem a go heng me
if a ketch him. Ohi –
All right Mrs. Williams, calm down
no need for all of that, he won't die.

Come here bwoy and let me see what happen
to your eye.
Ohi – ohi – ohi – a can't see mam.
Stop the bawling and come
hold up your head
you have a right to can't see
let me clean up the little blood.
Whoi – whoi –
See there just one tiny cut
not even near you eye.
Little cut
little blood
big mouth
plenty eye water and nuff nose-naught
big bwoy like you
coward no puss – cho –
See Joe here –
What really happen bwoy
tell me the truth –
I was fixing mi cart mam
and him come roun and was faasing wid it
and a tell him don't touch it
and same as him bend down
him head bounce pon the steering
and as him see the little blood him start bawl.
Is a accident and him is the cause –
Is not my fault at all.
See it stop bleeding
all this todo over nothing.
Hmm – hmm – hmm.
Look how you sen up mi pressure
and wase out mi cry
and nearly meck me commit murder
wait till I go home
you gwine pay fi roas and bwile.
A tell you all the while not to play
wid that big mout ugly bwoy
but you can't hear
so you must feel
you shoulda really blind.
You know what is true
gwaan home, move off from here

gwaan before me
and tek dat
whai –
till a come home
whai –
dat is di sample
whai –
dat is jus di brush
the curry comb deh a yard
a wait pon you
you hard earse brute
whai –

New Torshan

Aunt Gerty was a legend.
We children grew up on stories about this lady
proud to acknowledge her as relation.

She was proud and haughty
"From good stock – off a good table"
as she never failed to remind anyone
who would listen.
"My great grandfather
was the son of a white man
an estate owner
from Scotland.
And my great great granny by my mother side
was a Black Afrikain Princess
So me a no common marble."

The very way she say "Afrikain"
yu know she no ordinary.
Could be true because she
lived in the big old house
on Primenta Hill
and owned land as far as
your eyes could see.
The whole district
know her kindness
but also her wrath
for she never put up with foolishness.

In her younger days
so the story says
man follow her across the island for days
as she rode out on her grey mare.
She was tall and shapely
good looking and stately.
A lady who could pop a good joke
and knock back a glass a whites like any man.
She was a famous lady round about
but without a doubt
her greatest fame came because

she had more petticoat
than the law could read bout.
Petticoat wid lace of all description,
eyelet hole, tyrolese, embroidery, but mostly torshan.

Some say she had a hundred petticoats
some say five and twenty
all sorts of numbers.
No one know for sure
but it was plenty.
Every January – once a year
she wash dem, starch dem
and hang dem on the line till midnight.
They were something to behold
for she hang dem out all one time
and young and old marvel at the sight.

Stiff like buckram
white and pretty.
It take her a whole week to iron dem.
She wear dem three or four at a time
sometimes more
under the wide wide skirt
wid a tilta at the back.
When she walk pass
the tilta and the shif' dem move, dem say
side to side
up and down
wips – waps,
wips – waps.

It give nuff man trouble
young and old alike
in country and in town.
Well, is so mi granny tell me
I never see that part
for by the time I ole enough
to start know why man look pon woman
Aunt Gerty was "Granny Gerty"
and the walk was now low, slow
waddling like a duck
for age was a tek place.

FUN AND GAMES

We children
used to walk behind her
say we helping her over the hill to church
or up the step at the Doctor shop,
any where she going we behind her
pee pee cluck cluck.
For what we did want mos was
to hear the old time story
she and Miss Fan, her best fren
used to give out going up the hill.
That is how I come to know plenty things
like how Maas Caleb is not Glendon real father,
why Elder Jenkins lose the church a Back Pasture
and why dem call Teacher Powell "Sorry fi Puss".
The story dem juicy and rigin fi true
and Parson woulda read me out a church
if a tell most a dem to you
but I goin' tek a risk
and tell you just one little one
for you is mi good fren.
One Sunday
it was Easter time
we all going up the path to church
me and Percy and Man Man.
Granny Gerty and Aunty Fan
walking up ahead as usual
and ole time story a pop sweet cyaan done.

As we reach the little stream
at the foot of the second hill
we boys jump across
from stone to stone
to escape the mud mud –
Percy was in front of the old lady
I was in the back.
As Granny Gerty reach the stream
she pick up the frack
and the petticoat dem hoist dem above her waist
exposing the naked flesh no body suppose to see.

Aunty Fan was in shock.
"Gerty, a wha dat yu a do – behave yuself mam

yu noh see how yu expose! Shame!
See di pickney dem a laugh afta yu,
cho man, pull dung back yu clothes!"
"Mi dear Fan, yu can stay deh"
she say cool as cucumba
"Yu doan understan dis game
me noh waan no red mud
splash up pon mi slip dem
and mek dem spoil and stain."
"But yu expose yuself and mud will splash up yu bam-bam."
"Oh cho, Aunt Fan, yu is alright mi chile
better the bam bam splash up dan mi slip dem spoil,
is just last week I buy the torshan
yu know how long I have this ole backside."

Village Joke

Everybody know say
Miss Vie know say
her husband Luther fraid a duppy.

Everybody know say
Miss Vie know say
him deh wid her pretty fat niece.

But him didn't know
dat she know.
Him think nobody know.
For young gal skin
dazzle him brain
dim the ole fool eye.

So late one night
him leave home
to go meet her
at them secret spot.
Miss Vie ketch the rake
and follow at a distance
carrying two white sheet.
What happen next
had the whole district laughing
for many years to come.
Wrap up in the sheet dem
Miss Vie hide in the bush
as dem start to dweet
she rail up in front a dem
a real live duppy
tall and scary.

Luther jump up
lef de girl same place
lying in the grass
too frighten to move –
trousis in han
him bawl out in fright
and dung the road

From Behind The Counter

him run like pepper puss
into the pitch dark night.
Miss Vie behind him
one fi one
two fi two.
Two idle bwoy coming up the road
witness the whole thing
climb up on the high banking,
shouting and chanting
"run big fraid
little fraid back a yu
run big fraid
little fraid back a yu."

That was the chorus of the song
dem put dem eena.
Poor Mass Luther
from that day till today
the whole district change him name.
Not Luther as before,
but instead
everybody greet him
"run big fraid".

Married Story

Twenty-seven years
living, loving, sharing together,
and five children later,
Miss Cass a sedate quiet lady
live wid Maas Josh the butcher
an him know him have
one of the finest woman
who was his best friend and helpmate.
Every Friday and Saturday
dressed in her stiff starched bandana tie-head
and dainty apron to match
over her fresh floral skirt
she was in the butcher shop
head and head
helping Maas Josh.

So he married her in a pretty wedding
at the Anglican Church
one Wednesday in June
the year the war end.
Big nice wedding
plenty satin and lace
organdi and voile,
her two grand daughters
proudly holding up the veil.
Stepping wide to avoid the train
Maas Josh sporting a big smile
on his washed and powdered face,
was the happiest man alive.

Sunday turn thanks
another nice day
the couple look fresh as ever
Miss Cass in a pretty blue dress
with pink and white flowers
hat to match, shoes tu,
Maas Josh in a nice blue suit,
a nice pair of English leather boot
and a felt hat of velour gray
that him sister bring from England.

Next Friday bright and early
Miss Cass was on her way
to take her place
as usual in the meat shop.
But this was a different day
she was a different lady today,
don't you forget it,
she was mistress.
Mrs. Josiah Parish.

Today she leave the bandana tie-head
and the apron to match
and she was steppin
in Maas Josh English leather boot,
him white butcher apron
with the two deep pocket
and the grey felt hat
him sister from England bring.
And when she walk
the left han jus lef her side
and a float out swinging side to side
so all could see the wide gold ring
that make dem know
woman and man
mostly woman
that she was Mistress
and don't forget it
lawfully married.
All who doubt it
as if any one did
look pon de hat
the boot
the apron
and no wash over
the real thing,
the rahtid gold ring.

Gilnock Race Horse

Old Lennon took his place
on the long bench
in Mr. Lee's bar across from where
Mass Luther and brother Jack
Uncle Sam and Mr Rhoden were sitting.

Beside him was Baba C
Mass Bulla and Mr. Ankle.
They were exchanging stories for the past hour
then got around to horse racing.
Old Lennon who was the oldest of the lot
always had a good story
to top everyone else.

After a Q of whites
and much discussion
he took the floor.

"You think now-a-days horse can run?
Dem yah horse a donkey cubby
when you put dem side by side with ole time horse.
When me was a little bwoy inna short trousis
mi fadah used was to carry mi go a Gilnock fi watch horse race
only certain class a people could go there you know
but since mi fadah use to work fi dem,
we get een.
From day just a light out we leave home
and when we near Santa
you see the road busy with horse and buggy and moto car
on them way to Gilnock.
You see horse of all description
and class and condition,
under shady tree, under booth, under shed,
more and more horse a come een.
By the time racing fi start
is about a thousand of them
ready fi run.

A so di horse dem,
a so di people dem, all the man dem
dress up in coatie tail and top hat.
Di lady dem in a button up shoes,
broad hat and parasol,
shif, tilta, petticoat and shawl.
Den the bettin start.
Man a bet shilling, two-an-six, five shilling, ten shilling
Busha and de odder rich man dem a bet Guinea and Pound.
Big bet, little bet.
Man a bet two to one
five to one
twenty to one
and the place busy and noisy can't done.

As soon as the bettin settle dung fi every race
the jockey dem mount up
the bugle blow and di horse dem gone
roun and roun, roun and roun.
Man glad
nuff man sad
for dem bet out dem wife house money
what dem can't afford
a poor show great.

Well dis race day
I remember it was a
Easter Monday
me and mi fadah lef yard before day light
'Before cock put on him drawers' as mi granny say
and we reach Gilnock when sun hot.
Since mi fadah no have plenty money fi bet
we go roun whey di horse dem keep
and look and listen to what the groom and di jockey dem sayin.
If you want to know how fi bet a race course,
listen to groom and jockey, how dem talk
dem know more than owner man or anybody.

Well there was this pretty gray mare from Wesmalan
name Cusho Puss
and dem match her wid another mare
whey belong to the owner of the race course

a man name Mr. Densham.
Dem call that mare Red Gal.
The betting was strong pon di side of Red Gal
for to tell the truth, when you look pon di two a dem
it was like cheese to chalk.
For as pretty as Cusho Puss was,
she couldn't go up to Red Gal.

Jus as mi fadah decide to bet on Red Gal
a young man come up and whisper to him
'Bet on the gray, bet on the gray.'
Mi father run him and say
it look like the gray mare bruck dung already
and him not betting on no half dead horse.
Me was a mischevas little bwoy
and as mi fadah turn him back
mi follow the young man
go roun where dem have the horse dem
and hear him and another one talking say
dem pepper Cusho Puss
and dat the riding supple jack soak enna pepper fi nine days
an when the jockey lick wid dat
she gwine to fly like lightnin.

Well sir me did have fifteen shilling
me madder give me fi buy one leghorn Cock
and is like the devil kick me
me teck the money and buy not one, not two
but three ticket fi win offa Cusho Puss
five shillin a piece.
You can imagine how a nervous
when the bugle blow and the race start.
Red Gal jump into the lead one time.
Before you know it dem was coming roun the first turn
and when me look me nearly wet up mi self.
Cusho Puss a come dead last.
Me say lard, mi madder leghorn rooster fly gone now.
Cusho Puss a come dead last all the time, and a so me a fret
a so mi father a shout for fi him horse in front.
'Come Red Gal, run Red Gal, Red Gal' – me can barely call out
Cusho Puss, Cusho Puss.

All of a sudden as dem come roun fi start di last lap,
the jockey start drop lick with the pepper switch
an see ya sah,
Cusho Puss shoot off dung the track like a bullet.
She gellop pass all the other horse dem
and now she and Red Gal neck and neck,
heading towards the winning post.
Ah now mi voice strong – 'Cusho Puss! Cusho Puss!'
'Cusho Puss!'
a bawl tell a hoarse – 'Cusho Puss run Cusho Puss.'

The jockey git up eena di saddle
drop two bitch lick wid the pepper switch
and Cusho Puss shot pass Red Gal,
shot pass the winning post, an win di race.
Me glad so tell. Mr Densham nearly faintway,
for the betting was heavy.
But a yah so de prekke begin,
For when the jockey try fi pull her up
Cusho Puss wouldn't stop
so di pepper a bun so di mare a run
the poor jockey can't stop her.
Di owner of the horse nearly mad
people run after dem, no help.
A man jump pon a horse a try fi ketch dem
an haffi turn back
the mare a gellop same way.
Some little bwoy up in a robin mango tree start chant out
'Horse a gellop and di man can't pull him back
ride him jockey, ride him bwoy.'

You never see so much excitement from you born.
Sometime after that we hear say the jockey manage fi slip off
somewhere dung a Santa Bottom, widout any serious injury
and Cusho Puss never stop gellop
till him reach him master yard
way dung a Wesmalan.
A deh dem go fine him the next day when dem reach home,
under the guango tree whey dem usually tie im.
Aih sah – dat was a day.

FUN AND GAMES 105

Say you want to know what happen to the ticket dem me buy?
Me tell mi fadah bout the ticket dem
and is the fus time mi fadah ever hug me up.
We colleck wi winnings seven poun ten shillings.
Him give me five shillings fi mi self,
an I reach heaven same time
him teck one poun fi im self,
and him and him frien dem drink up.
We buy the leghorn rooster fi mi madda,
an a hen to match fi brawta
and him buy up tings fi mi sister dem.

We reach home dat night full a liquor and food
and mi fadah meck me promise
dat me wouldna teck dem kine a chance again
and him promise not to tell mi madda.
From dat day me an him was bes fren,
specially like how him teck the balance of the money
and buy a pretty likkle heffer fi me
according to him
to meck me into a man.

But if a live till a dead
I will never forget the day – mi fadah a call fi Red Gal,
'Run Red Gal, run Red Gal, run Red Gal,'
me a bawl out, 'Cusho Puss, Cusho Puss, run Cusho Puss.'
And the little bwoy dem
a Gilnock race course eena di Robin mango tree a chant,
'Horse a gellop and di man can't pull him back
Ride him jockey, ride him bwoy.
Horse a gellop and di man can't pull him back
Ride him jockey, ride him bwoy.'"

Married Yes

Say what?
Baxside!
Missa Jackson a go married!
What no happen in a year
happen in a day –
Look how long him deh a worl,
look how much pickney him get,
look how much woman him fool
well sir I neva see nothing so yet
Missa Jackson can barely walk
and can't move an inch
without the walking stick,
arthritis in him joint dem
and him hafi noint dung every night with healing oil.
But if you ask him how dat go
him always ready with the answer
"I am getting married yes,
after all is only my foot that is sick".

Wedding Belle

In the church on the hill
on a Wednesday in June
Mr. Young married Miss Bell
with flowers white veil
and a white satin gown edged with lace
purchased at a ready-made store in town
organ music, solo singing
bridesmaids bestman flower girls
all the fancy trimmings you could tell
it was the talk for months
the district had never seen anything so grand
and flocked to the church
just to be on hand to witness the event
and cheer the couple on.
In the best tradition and customary style
attended by her daughters and grand ones too
she wore
something old something new
something borrowed something blue.
Walking up the aisle on her brother's arm
she was a picture of mature loveliness and charm.
She said her "I do" in voice strong and clear
and at the right moment shed a few modest tears
dabbed with a 'kerchief of delicate white lace
avoiding the powder and rouge on her face.
Seeing her then you would never believe
they had lived together as man and wife
for more than thirty long years.

Serious Things

Plain Truth

Look here nuh
I know yuh long time
so don't mek mi rude to yuh
an go on bad
so shame mi mother.
What yuh mean by doh . . .
you muss be really jokin,
or is something bad yuh was smokin.

Is just too too sad
if dat is all you have to say,
for yuh no know me as no leggo . . .
not one bit,
nor no pick-up-a-street girl.
Yuh know me in mi father house . . .
Is only two room but a fi wi hit
for doh we poor
we not pauperise.
Though I might joke wid you
that is not leave nor licence
for you to take no liberty wid me.

I know some girls would be glad
for the opportunity
to socialise and familiarise,
but not me.
So understand one thing straight and plain,
and don't let me have to tell you again.
If that is all you have to say,
save yuh breath and don't bother
for if me not good enough to be a wife
me no want to be nobody baby mother.

Day Light Out

If ever day light out
in the middle of the night
you know what it would reveal?
Because the blanket of the night
much evil and badness conceal you know,
and if all the truth were known
about everybody and everyone
think what this would do
to the high and mighty
the meek and lovely
if moon suddenly turn into sun.

But sad to say
that will never be
people born and live and die
go to their graves believing one thing
when something else is the truth
the whole truth and nothing but.

Hear these two cases and
your own conclusions make
of two young men like many you know
who father children
and leave the mothers behind alone
to face the burden
and many a sad young girl
is still in school when she get the fall
that blight her life for ever.

Corporal Douglas was a respectable man
married the nurse at the clinic
settled down with three children
the district respected the corporal
now nearing forty years old.
But when he was eighteen in police training
"fall" Mavis Anglin age sixteen still in school.

He disappeared as you could guess.
She "bring" the child

was a nice little boy.
She tried her best
but the nice little boy turned bad
no father to scold him
 to love him and hold him
to train and counsel the lad.

Now years later on duty one night
Corporal Douglas arrested a boy
for crime and violence and badness galore.
The corporal knew it was a gang affair
but the young man wouldn't speak
so the good corporal used the baton with good effect
till at last the boy showed proper respect.

And if that midnight darkness turned to light
you can imagine the corporal's plight.
The said boy bleeding on the concrete
at the respectable corporal's feet
was the said Mavis child
by the said corporal
respectable man
who married the nurse at the clinic
twenty years ago.
Oh God if I did know
if I did know.

The second story is no different.
From Bobby was a youth
he was a charmer — sweet boy
and as he grew —
every girl's parents knew
that he took what he wanted with such smile and charm
and so he thought no harm done
that's life.
One night when he was about twenty
and the school had a dance
he way-laid pretty Blossom
the girl who lived with her granny on the hill
and the poor virgin girl couldn't say no
he charmed her so
with the sweetest lyrics

no DJ ever dream about
that boy had such a sweet mouth.

But when the baby came he disappeared
some say to foreign never to return.
The little baby pretty like money
and the young mother died giving birth
but lived long enough to name her Honey.
The pretty little angel – fatherless, motherless
who resembled her dead mother
lived with her greatgran
until a lady took her to Kingston
when greatgran passed on
not so long after.
She worked with the lady
in her bar on Sutton Street
grew up pretty and sweet
and reached the tender age of seventeen
nice and neat.

One night a man came in
talking with a foreign accent
with plenty money, gold jewellery
and fancy clothes.
He charmed the young miss
invited her out
she couldn't resist
he had such a sweet mouth
with more lyrics than a DJ ever dream about.

She gladly said yes for he made promises to no end
he liked younger girls, would treat her real well
so they ended up in Negril in a fancy hotel.
Well he wined her, dined her
bought her presents galore
and so on, so forth and even so fifth,
sixth, seventh and then some more.
She pleased him he said
as he turned to her in the bed
and enquired from where she came and her full name
for strangely he thought she brought to his mind
someone he knew long ago.

Serious Things   113

And if that midnight darkness turned to light
and it was broad day in the middle of that night
you can imagine this old brute's plight,
his said bed mate was the said little Honey
born to the said Blossom eighteen years ago.
What's done can't be undone . . .
But oh God if I did know
if I did know.

Journey

I entered this world
not of my own choosing.
Somewhere, somehow, someone
dictated what form my body would take,
what colour eyes, hair, skin,
how tall, what weight,
what joys I would know,
what pain I would endure,
what songs my soul would sing,
and what turbulent waters
I would cross to reach the shore,
carefully planned to the last minute detail.

So I stand in this life
who I am, what I am
fashioned by the hand that
made the trees,
the flowers, the fires, the waters,
each for its own purpose – separate,
together to fulfill a greater plan.
And with this knowledge
to the dictates of the creator
I sing the songs
forever constant in my being
and dance to the rhythm of their compelling music
never a beat, a moment losing
for I know soon, all too soon
I shall leave all this behind
depart this world
as I came,
not of my own choosing.

Word is Wind

All right,
I hear you
loud and clear
on radio and
on Tee Vee
over foreign country
and "Back a Yard",
you never have it hard
to find the words to state your case.
For example, Sir, and there are many such,
you tell the Youth Conference
about Parliamentary Democracy and Alien Ideology.
You tell the Festival
about Cultural Heritage and Ancestry,
you tell the Nation
about Inflation,
Balance of Payments,
Gross National Product
and the Ladder of Expectation.
About Upliftment and Economic Recovery,
about Development Strategy
and Basic Motivational Philosophy.
Nice words, my friend, nice.
You don't think twice
to drop in Structural Re-adjustment,
Re-development, Divestment, and De-regulation.
You talk about the Basin Plan
you get from the American
for the elevation of the Caribbean.
And the Can to match from the other man.
Caribbean Basin, Carib Can.
Big words, little words, nice words,
no mind we don't understand.
Words, words, words – for all and any occasion.
And they say you bright – right? Right!
So I have one simple question
tell me – tell me Sir please,
how do you tell a hungry child goodnight?

Plaiting Song

The curly haired boy
with deep green-grey eyes
sits by the lantern light
plaiting straw for pretty hats.
He sings a mischievous song
each naughty note, sweet
drips from his sensuous lips
full, dark-pink, wet.
Goose bumps rise on necks and arms
of those around pretending work.
His open handsome face
burnished by the amber light
tells of Spanish ships
native peoples
ebon bodies dripping sweat
marked by savage whips.
Deftly his strong, long fingers
weave the silver thatch
the finished braid uncoiling
like a yellow snake disturbed,
growing between his thick strong
honey coloured thighs
falling to the jute bag on the ground.
He sings and plaits, plaits and sings
unaware of the fires he kindles,
the stirrings his being evokes,
for he does not know
among those who watch
there's one who loves him
more than he loves himself.

Message From an Old Man

(for Eddie Burke)

As I sit here
where somebody put me
warming the morning sun
I have a rememberance
now mi working days done –
that take me back
to those days long gone
when I was strong
hearty and young
up and about
and did the work of three man
me one.

I work from sun up to sun dung
seven days a week
twelve months a year,
for many many years
with muscle and brain.
God gave the strength
I believe in his might
I could do anything,
go to any length.
I answered any call
morning, noon or night,
without counting the cost.
I didn't stop to think of mi family
those who love me –
not even mi self.
Oh yes I travel the island
I travel the world
and the work I do
is a legend today,
most times with insufficient pay.
I think I could never stop,
that I would go on forever.

See me now
I sit here
a useless frame
sometimes not even
remembering mi own name,
a faint shadow
of the man I was
doing everything like a little baby again.
Once a man
painfully true,
twice a child.
One thing I don't forget
give thanks and thank the giver.

So I give you young man
young lady,
and all who will heed
so you don't have
mi one regret,
a piece of advice
all for free,
so take it freely
from a weary old man.

Take a little time for yourself
time with you family
smell the flowers
walk in the rain,
talk to the birds
and God's other creatures.
Savor the pleasure
feel the pain
live, love, laugh a while
and dance if you feel like it,
laugh and cry again.
Play and run and sing
and laugh with the children,
all those who love you.
Sometime, take the time
just to be by yourself
and do nothing, nothing
except count you blessings

and give thanks.
For soon, too soon it will pass,
and you're on the other shore,
you see no more
hear no more
feel no more, no more.

Village Tragedy

Miss Gladys
Maas Percy long time wife
tired of the pain
and the shameful strife
buy a ready made dress
with the prementa money
him saving to buy the next mule.
Dress to puss back foot
she find herself
down by young Belle gate
where she know
her husband visit regular
and stay late,
just so she could brag.

The whole district laugh again
for Belle long decide to stop roaming
and was away in the nursing home
giving birth to Maas Percy twins
a pigin pair
girl and boy.

That night as Miss Gladys land back home
Maas Percy drop lick in her side
not for the mule money she spen
though him buy the new rope already,
but ascording to him
she shouldn't lower herself to that
she had no pride.

Belle was only a vessel for the seed
a hole you dig and plant and breed.
So him say twisting the knife deep deep
in the pain of her barren womb.

She weep for a week.
He wasn't there to see,
just waiting every day
for the babies to smile

at their over middle-age father.
Him head swell big
and him walk with a strut
after all him was man.

Friday afternoon Miss Gladys disappear
lost cawn fine.

The whole village search
till Sunday morning
just when first bell a ring
at the old Church on the hill,
dem fine Miss Gladys a swing
from the low guango limb,
the new mule rope tight round her neck
stopping her shame and her grief.

The shock send Maas Percy
straight to bed
him couldn't believe
him wife dead
and up to now
him don't stop cry.
Up to now
him don't know why,
for all him can do now,
is mumble to himself,
"How she could do me dat,
how she could do me dat,
teck her owna life,
after all
she was mi lawful married wife,
mi lawful married wife."

A Woman's Prayer for Shelter

A roof over my head
Lord
a little house
with two windows
and a door I can lock
so I can feel secure
and don't ever have to move no more.
A house with a lamp and a clock.
A little house Lord,
with a tiny yard
few flowers a croton a mint,
a lime and a pepper tree,
where I can invite you in
and talk together in privacy
anytime.
A house to call my own,
for I really tired to roam.
Lord without a house
how can I make a home?

Outside Pickney

Sunday eena church
Miss Constance whisper behind the hymn book
as her brother outside son,
whey look like him, walk een
"You know Miss Vie,
something always puzzle me,
is how fate play strange games wid some a we.
Take mi brodder
who try fi hide the fact
that him is the father,
when the bwoy come out
the very dabs a him."

It always happen
and plenty man
rich or poor, high or low
meet the same drop
as if fi spite
even when dem deny it
you cut off the chile head
and put dem side by side
di one dem try to hide,
is the spitting image.
Look at mi nephew,
the bwoy fava the father can't done,
down to the very squint in him lef eye.
A tell you when im say
the pickney a no fi him
a lie him lie.
It no right
for him did go deh,
that's why name call.
As mi granny always say
what done in a darkness
bound to come out eena light,
and some things just can't hide
and is a warning
to man and woman alike
what you set at night time
tan tuddy till morning light.

No Tears for the Wicked

Busha dead.
Busha dead?
Busha White dead,
dead as nit.
Well I am not a hypocrite
I don't sorry one damn.
I not saying a glad mark you
for death is fi all a wi
as you born you start the journey
and God's word must come to pass
but me shedding no tears for him
for Busha was a wicked rass.

Pay Day Decision

Look pon di wages
whole week a work
only twelve and six me get.
What dat can do for a big man like me
who have so much responsibility
in a di Big Christmas?
By the time me pay Missa Chin
give Mavis the baby supportance
an Louise and Agnes to
pay fi di file and the cutlass
all I end up wid is four shilling an fuppance.
What the ass!!
Me don't even buy a white rum yet.
What a bitch of a life
and mi wife a yard a look
her two pickney dem
want new clothes, fee fee and exercise book.
Well, to hell wid all dat
Me can't work so hard and don't enjoy miself
just done wid that kinda chat.
Every Jack man and woman have to wait
those outside and those a yard
me have to spree myself and feel good
after all me is de man.
Good will to all man
dat mean me tu,
if anything lef after me done drink mi liquor
dem will hafi satisfy
dat will have to do.

Mosquitos

Big like horsefly
bite like sandfly
plenty like gingyfly
mosquitoes
fly and sing
pitch and sting
whole blessed night
boxing and clapping
stomping and slapping
no sleep no dreams
only the deaf escapes it seems.
No spray, no smoke stops the attack,
in daylight same thing
mosquitoes galore
non-stop, more and more
front and back
fly and sing
pitch and sting
then you can tell
he from she
male from female
the deadlier of the species
mosquitoes –
wicked thing.

Tracings

Don't provoke mi peace this morning
ah just done say mi prayers
you are interfering, fast and out of order
to say those things about mi one sister
so this to you is a warning.
Yes me and mi sister have a fuss
but what is that to you?
Me and mi sister affair is no concern to you
or anybody else you hear.

Right now we disagree
that is wi privilege, wi right
but that don't give you any leave or license
to pass your dirty remarks about her pedigree.
You no response fi wi quarrel.
Even if we fight no take that up pon you head
you no have no cotta, no vessel
no box, no barrel big enough for that
you neck no strong enough to carry that load
it bigger than you,
so put it dung right ya so.
You don't see blood thicker than water
you no see that's why you can't prosper
you ole eye them fava toad.
You know what is your trouble
you know what is the matter
all the while
you siddung a fan fly off a other people cow head
and leave your own fi spoil.

Teck dis to you bed. Hear mi foolish advice
leave people affairs alone,
and cover you over active mouth
or one a dese days so help me you gwine sorry,
for if a don't ketch you in the jigging,
I bound to ketch you in the reeling.
If a don't ketch you in the quadrille
bet you old boot bottom I will ketch you in the polka.
Face fava when rainy weather
buck up pon middle year drought.

128 *From Behind The Counter*

Perception

Blindly we cling to the things we perceive
till we come to believe them explicitly
as gospel even.

We hang our beliefs about ourselves
ornaments of our flawed reasoning
or with them wrap our fragile egos
admitting no humility,
no discussion,
no possibility of error
allowing few other points of view,
even then ours are always right.
Our arrogance and conceit so nurtured grows
as we see ourselves as demigods.

How sad the time we waste
in such vainglorious activity
how much we lose
of truth and of reality.

Strategy

It rough, caan rougher.
Tough, caan tougher.
From we foreparents ship come
we under the whip
Backra Massa keep we under subjection,
without language without drum.
But we nah give up
no matter how it get bad, we caan give up
for one day, one day it have to stop.
Massa God nah sleep.
So we fight the battle day by day, little by little
if you caan run you walk, caan walk you creep,
caan talk, you sing, do something
for if we don't win the battle we lose the war.

So hear the plan,
apart from everything else
this yah one belongs to we woman
so no tell no man for dem won't understand.
Some a di Busha dem love black flesh,
even if them beat you a day, you bet
when bedtime come is a different thing
is like them skin ketch fire
and rub butter a puss mouth im bound to lick it –
no fret.

So hear the older head –
You see like how dem say young Busha never brush yet,
when you serve him the wine under-look him,
roll you eye dem in a dem socket, them pretty enough.
Spill the wine pon him trousers front right deh
walk with you serving napkin in a you pocket
and when you wipe it, press you hand pan him private
that guarantee him gwine call you to him room
for him think you want it.
When you get in a him bed
shut you eye tight, grit you teeth
and wine you waist gal
meck him leggo every thing give you,

for all you want is a brown baby
that guarantee privilege and the more the merrier.
Is a sure way fi start teck whey Backra power.
If you caan ketch him in the reeling
one night, one night
you ketch him in a the jigging.

Doesn't it Matter

Doesn't matter who the gunman is
   – he is
Doesn't matter who gave the gun in his hand
   – it is loaded
Doesn't matter where the bullet in the loaded gun
in his hand came from
   – it is there
Doesn't matter why he will pull the trigger
to fire the bullet
in the gun in his hand
   – he will.

Perhaps for no reason
except, every day is hunting season
for what he may get
to feed his need or greed.
The bullet in the gun in his hand
is marked with death.
Doesn't matter whose death.

It is someone's life, a human person.
Your life, my life, all life.
Doesn't matter if we end up in heaven or in hell
every gunman is a threat to the life of everyone
hear and mark that well
then ask yourself
doesn't it matter?

Cane Piece Blues

Sugar cane, sugar cane
sweet sugar cane
green fields stretching arrowing for miles
with a myriad secret places
where my falla-line father
with bewitching smiles
took my innocent mother
under the sun tying bundles
near the end of the crop
promising to return next year.
Busha riding through near near
counting rows of tons
not seeing my mother
making sons and daughters
with seasonal crop time cutters.
Sugar cane, sugar cane
sweet sugar cane turned sour vinegar,
and my mother
old before her time.

Sugar cane, sugar cane
intoxicating pungent
fresh-cut under hot sun
like my father took my mother
the handsome stranger took me
promising to return next year
the same promise
year after year, years upon years
whispered in innocent trusting ears.

Scarcely knowing what was happening
fighting back the burning tears
I exchanged my maiden head and innocence
for a pumpkin belly growing
growing with the seed he planted
digging with selfish cruelty.
Sugar cane, sugar cane
stretching green, arrowing for miles
where now I sit to hide my swelling shame

wondering if he really will come back
sitting like my mother, expecting
sucking bitter sorrow and blame.
Sugar cane, sweet sugar cane
watching red ants carry a piece of trash
down, down through the long winding crack
and my eye-water falling, falling, falling
does not soften
the hard unforgiving earth.

Advice

Say what?
Him beat you again?
When?
Night before last, last night
and last week Sunday.
The week before
and the week before that.
Once, some time two time a week.
You no tired fi teck lick.
You no tired of the shame
and batteration?
Why you don't leave
the old mampala man
and go look you owna living?
Look how you mawga an tan.
Look pon you head.
Look pon you close.
You no shame of yourself?
Dis time is you han him bruck
you want to know the trute
next time maybe is you neck.
A the food him beat you for last night?
Wicked brute!
If you cook him beat you
you no cook him beat you
so don't cook one damn
no give the wretch
nutten fi nyam.

Days when man a batter woman fi stop.
One day you a go drop dung dead
and what will happen to you
two pickney dem?
So you take my foolish advice –
Lef him –
You can do better dan dat.
You don't even reach thirty yet
tree no grow eena you face
him no put ring pon you finger

no chain no round you neck
tek you two pickney an go bout you business
and don't come back
no matter how him beg –
damn disgrace –
no meck him teck you meck no foot cloth
nor no beating post
for what you a get from him
plenty man have better
an you name woman
you have you whey
and you a somebody pickney
so lef him
lef him an goo wey.

Senseless

. . . and yet they come
bearing weapons of war
killing killing . . .
unwilling victims die
not knowing why their lives were stilled
and they who gave the death
knew not who or why they killed . . .

From the Sidelines

I have drunk
much of life's wine.
I have walked in front
I've walked behind.
Now from the sidelines
I watch the parade go by
one thing in all this I've learnt,
it pays us all
to be gentle and kind.

Getting On

(for Jean)

    So the light gently grows dim
    a little dimmer
    the climbing grows steep
    a little steeper
    the steps get short
    a little shorter
    and memories elude us now
    those we would most recall.
    But the love grows stronger deeper
    nurtured by the sharing
    watered by the tears of sorrow, joy too
    the pain and ecstasy of the caring
    for so we mark the passing years
    shedding our passions and our fears.

I saw my Land

Take a next look

Every day pass
weeks pass
months and years pass
ages pass . . .
Like we
passing cross hills
with trees tall and stately
short and shapely
down valleys deep wide steep.
Passing by bright-colour flowers
and cool mountain rivers
where ticky-ticky and tadpole
play hide-and-seek.
Where sun take too long to reach a morning time
and moon can barely touch the soft grass below
sake a plenty vine and green leaf overhead . . .
Where bamboo tree dance in the crisp-crisp breeze
with pretty brown-skin gal in print-cotton chemise . . .
Passing beside little ramshackle house
with too much pickney
playing in the loose dirt
not enough to eat, and naked
except for the one old shirt hanging
like wis-wis pon dry guango tree . . .
passing dig-up dig-up road
where careless driver leave the motor car carcass
pass the wall the politician mess up
pass the bruck-down school-house dem don't fix up,
passing into dirty street where last week garbage
and one dead dog meet to breed
fly and pestilence
crime and violence . . .
Where costly hate and free love
hide and fornicate behind a rusty zinc fence.
Yes every day pass
and ages pass
and we pass
and shut wi eye
make say we don't see

neither pretty nor ugly
scattered round we
greater than any story book.
Look man
Open yuh eye . . .
Look again . . .
Take a next look.

The River

(for Owen Minott)

The river begins
first a tiny drop
somewhere high up in the mountain top
then gathers millions as it flows
on its winding way across the land
watering the fields
animals and weeds
watering the seeds
nurturing the yields
giving food
giving life
fashioning the beauty
of flowers, trees
and people
the lovely, bold people
young, old, not so old.

Now gentle river crystal clear
a mother rocking her baby to sleep.
Then rough, muddy
turbulent, swift, dangerous and deep
a warlord, angry, sweeping all before it
leaving everything bare
and life at the riverside that time –
tough.
The river washes
our clothes
our bodies
our souls
healing stream, Alleluia
as we gather
river beautiful
life giver, life taker
flowing ever
to the endless, eternal sea . . .
how like life . . .
the river.

Under Banyan Tree

This country grows in your gut
like a Banyan tree
spreading strong limbs of hurt and happiness
reaching in the far corners of your insides.
Each branch drops a thousand roots
that knot up your belly bit by bit
tangle your heart-string
and the only thing you can do
is love it.
You find yourself going and coming,
now you love, now you hate and love again
"Me da rock so, you da rock so".
You can't escape it
even when you curse it go away
green-card it to
country grade AA
stow away to the "Mother Land"
or any other place,
the pain and love in your gut get worse and worse.
You can't understand
for the big fat purse
is no pain killer – no mind healer
"For you da rock so, me da rock so!"
God Almighty!
How do you leave a lover
you know since you know yourself?
Since the first stirring?
You keep remembering the heaven and the hell
the sweetness and the gall
the long nights
the cool days
the hot loving, burning
the fight and the quarrel
the leaving, the returning
and the peace . . .
What is it, what is it
will it ever cease?
You don't really want it stop
for this is your life,

the misery, the mystery of it.
More and more the Banyan roots
tighten round your feet
and your heart strings
move into your brain
anchor you to the bedrock
till you become the root,
the tree – the rock itself
you're one with the root
the tree and the rock.
And you know the only place
you'll go in your bed in your head
is six feet under.
"You da rock so
me da rock so
under Banyan tree."

Consolation

You who boldly defied the odds
unlocked the doors
tore away the impregnable bars
ignoring deep hurting scars
allowing the caged ones
escape to freedom and self,
you watching in their early days
as timidly they moved
first with halting steps unsure
cautiously into light
gaining strength and worth,
do not despair now in your closing years
that you see their offspring
in their new estate, your legacy,
in their zeal
it seems trampling the very freedom-seeds
you so devotedly sowed
and watered with your sweat and tears.
They live in your dreams remember
it was for them your heirs
you toiled often in the dark.
As they find the light
they will find their way
stumble, fall, lose the mark
but find it again in joy and pain
believing, accomplishing, achieving
in their own time
in their own place
at their own pace.
Perhaps they forget you
as you sometimes regret
but yet in time, in time
there are praise-songs
to warm ancestral hearts
and time is an eternity.

Dark Night

No moon tonight
the cloud hides the stars
thick darkness
blacks out the trees,
shrubs, houses, church building,
telegraph poles,
everything.
Fireflies
shine their way through
flashing invitations
to seeking mates,
sounds of crickets and toads
signal their way
in time with their pulsing light.
An out-of-tune banjo
coming by the cross roads
picks out a plaintive melody,
the players' feet on the gravel road
marks the time
in perfect rhythm
sweeting the ear.

Corn Time

You don't remember when
we use to grow wi own corn?
Well let me tell you.
All over Jamaica dem time, so,
you see corn field
pretty like any money
big and small, on hillside and level
long before plenty of you born.

When you hear crop time
what a nice time.
Besides the cash it bring een
the nice corn food we get,
better yet –
corn is something that keep
family and friends together,
living, working in harmony.
Planting time we make morning sport.
Me give you day
you give me day,
we give one another day fe day.
When we working we singing
old time songs ringing,
from wi granny memory
mix wid sankey,
chorus and hymns
ancient and modern.
Food boiling
people toiling,
love flowing,
corn growing.

When dem ripe
roast corn,
bwile corn,
parch corn,
plenty corn-eating.
Night time
we play ship sail

sail fast, how many men,
old and young alike
fun and games,
it was nice then.

Plenty time
breakfast or supper
was smooth green corn porridge,
rough corn pone
or stick in de ribs corn dumpling,
holding you up
like concrete mortar.

Crop time now
we reap before the rain come dung.
In buttery
under zinc pon barbecue
under thatch we well busy.
Night after night we gather together
sometime till morning light
for shelling match.
Man and woman,
boys and girls,
old and young
test speed and skill,
who can shell the most.
We sing and tell nuff joke
or the biggest lie.
Nuff story telling
nuff corn shelling
nuff nuff laughing
nuff riddle guessing.
Round the rugged rock
the ragged rascal ran,
never mind the blister on your han,
how many r's in dat.
Heaps of the prettiest corn, newly reaped
red and yellow
separate fast from trash
cob and stick
with steady hands
of friends and family moving quick,

as if by magic
change to big basket full
to plant next crop.
Crocus bags fill up
ready for market.
Will feed horse
feed cow
feed fowl
feed pigeon.
But best part of all,
is the two full doona pan leave back
to make –
hell a top hell a bottom
alleluia pone and dumpling
hominy and asham.
Yes sir, yes ma'am,
corn time
nice time!

Drought

Everything dry up.
The whole place dry dry.
No rain falling
drought almost a year.
Everyone praying for rain.
Everybody calling
for water, rain-water.
Suddenly thunder clap
clouds grow dark dark
rain drop
for days none stop.
In no time
everything wet up
everywhere wet wet.
Now everyone
everybody praying hard hard
praying for rain to stop.

The Rain

The place is dry.
Dry, dry.
Flowers, trees and leaves
parched to brown curly crispness
in country in town.
Streams no longer flow
some disappear totally
or dried to a mere trickle.
Ponds are dried out mud
hard cracked clay mosaics
under the hot sun
bearing down all day.
For a year almost, no rain.
Birds, bees, butterflies travel miles
for the tiniest sip
cows, horses, donkeys, goats
children too with dirty faces
find no drink in the usual places.
Suddenly a darkening cloud
a clap of thunder deafening loud
as the heavens open
and the rains come down.
Buckets, pails, pots and pans
drums and barrels fill up,
full full, overflow.
Birds, bees, butterflies,
horses, donkeys, cows, goats
all living things
drink the cooling soothing
quenching rain-water.
In no time everything wet wet.
Trees bow low as welcome raindrops
fill each leaf and stem
children screaming with delight
run out into the pouring rain
playing in the rain
laughing in the rain
falling in the rain
falling in the yard,
sliding into brown thick mud mud.

Small Eyes

Aunt Sue's house was in my childhood eyes
large and spacious.
A wide wide verandah
ran right across the front,
and the roof rose majestically to the skies.
Glass sash windows
let the sunlight
into three bedrooms, large sitting hall,
dining room and pantry.
At the back a wide wide porch
caught the evening shadow
making a gathering place large, cool and inviting.
We could even crawl underneath the house-bottom
to collect fowl-eggs, puppies and chickens
and retrieve our ball and gig,
the house in our small wondering eyes
was a mansion big, big, big.
Now today through grownup eyes mature
the large old house huge and grand
is a small humble place
can you understand?
Even Aunt Sue's towering figure
seems smaller now than before
and the wide wide verandah
where we rolled and played and ran wild
is not half as wide anymore.
So it is
So it is
In the eyes of a child the small seems great.
In the eyes of the weak
small difficulties seem enormous
and all prospects dim and bleak.

Music Man

Sitting on the woodpile out in the yard
he gaily strums his banjo out of tune.
He doesn't mind, it pleases his tone deaf ears
and his chief listener is the old man in the moon.
You'll find he is deaf too,
how else would he all these years
ignore the yelping dog behind him
and all the earth dogs howling every night
in and out of their season
and the music man's out of tune forever music.
For song after song he strums and sings
through the whole night long
for many moons and many more tunes,
on the banjo he chopped out of a cedar stump.
If you happen to pass and catch a snatch of a melody
you recognize and want to sing
remember move up or down half a tone
and do your best not to be seen by him,
my friend will want you to remain forever
and to the out of tune ordeal there will be no end.
In his head you see he is a music man
different, you understand from a musician.

Negril Sunset

I have seen sunsets
on the Mediterranean,
on the warm waters
of the Southern Caribbean.
Sunsets in the Americas
north and south.
In the far east and down under
in the lands of Bible times,
west of east around the globe.
Sunsets that would all your senses fill
but never one to match
the Sunset in September
in Jamaica at Negril.

Mere Mortals

I have sworn myself a lover
of warm golden sunsets
cool drizzly mornings
marking rainbows
against the lush green of my native hillsides
glowing in new sunlight;
of meadows soft,
cooled by the gentlest breeze
rolling down to the bluest sea
you have ever seen,
waiting to float the dying sun-god
daily 'round the globe
as early stars in growing numbers
twinkle in the delight of deep blue skies.
We are so tiny, we poor mortals
set side by side
with mountain, sea, stars and rainbows.
To think otherwise
than we are mere playthings of the creator,
all be it the favourites,
is presumption and utter folly.
For mountain, sea, stars and rainbows
will be here long long after
we have all gone
like a breath of wind
through the trees,
across the grass
over the water.

Santa Cruz – Holy Cross

(for Fr. Richard & Santa Friends)

Santa Cruz
Holy Cross
Santa Santa Cruz
echoes of Spanish ships
memories of strange men
with flags, swords and whips
friars holding up bible and crucifix
symbols of their intent,
minds set, walking pristine islands
among natives semi-clad
living close to nature and to God
oblivious of Isabella and Ferdinand
Catholic Majesties sporting Christian Creed
heaven bent
yet anxious to satisfy their greed
for loot and gold.
Crude men
bringing disease pestilence and death
gave this place the name
Santa Cruz Holy Cross
Santa Santa Cruz.
Those same brutal men
savages from across the ocean seas
brought also news of another life,
for out of the evil of Spanish ravages and conquest
came the gospel of salvation
everlasting life eternal rest
wrought by the cross, the Holy cross
de Jesus Christo Salvador
Santa Santa Cruz
of Jesus Christ the saviour.
In one hand the men of Spain carried the gospel of life
evidenced in Holy writ
in the other the implement of destruction
death and strife.
Even now how much are we different
from the conquistadors?

What do we carry in our hands
to the innocent and trusting?
Sad sad the natives died at Spanish hands
not knowing the meaning of the well-intentioned gift,
sadder yet so few among us now acknowledge the worth
the symbol of our ransom and rebirth
who in these lands truly sing the praises of the cross
Holy Cross, Santa Cruz.
So we ask you now Señor Dios Padre draw near,
hear the thanks we bring to you father God
for the glory of the cross the Holy Cross
Santa Santa Cruz.
Gracias Gracias Señor Gracias a Dios
Por Jesus Christo Salvador,
for Jesus Christ the Saviour,
thanks and thanks again.
By the mercy of His Cross, the Holy Cross
Santa Cruz, Santa Cruz
have mercy on us penitents
for our omission, our commission.
Ten piedad de nosotros
have mercy on us and the Spanish Señores
by the power of the Cross the Holy Cross
Santa Santa Cruz.
Have mercy, have mercy
for still in imitation of the men of Spain
we lift high and strong the hand of death
hiding the life-hand of the Saviour
Santa Salvador Jesus Christo.
Ten Piedad – Ten Piedad
Have mercy, have mercy on us
forgive us all by the power of your Cross
Holy Cross Santa Santa Cruz.

In the Park, Up-Town, Down-Town

Lord!
What a way the place pretty
flowers,
shade trees,
nuff birds and bees.

Concrete bench
coulda mek fifty house
and water fountain
spraying high in the air.
I coulda bathe inna that
amount a water for ten year
judge by the two butter pan full
I have to use
two time a week.
Can't even wash as far as possible sometime
for the pan leak.
But lawd the place
nice fi true
new – clean – lovely to kill,
must be so heaven stay.
I coulda sit here the whole, blessed day,
but Lord,
a hungry so till.

Town Clock

Busha built a clock tower
in the middle of town
where two main roads crossed
one going up
one going down
in memory so he says
of his dear sweet wife.
For those who didn't know her
it didn't matter in the next
nor in this life.
And whoever knew her
won't care a row of pins
always listing her sins
against the poor.
For she was a hard cruel woman
who had no sympathy
gave no quarter
and if the truth be told
not even to her one son and daughter.
So Busha and his clock can stay evermore
he could sweet talk till kingdom come
till stars even start to drop
for in any case it only works sometimes
most times the dumb clock stop.

By the Sun

You can stay there
say you working by the clock.
Me?
I work by the sun
sun up to sun down
and get through more than you can.
Every watch or clock
sometimes work and stop
but sun rise and set
every blessed day from time immemorial
without pausing or stopping.
Take my advice
work by the sun
you get much much more done.

Introduction

It affords me much pleasure Sir Excellency
to make your honourable acquaintance
and to welcome you most heartily
on the behalf of the whole districts
of Donebeholden and Content
and on the behalf of my own behalf.
My name is Jasper Azariah Altiman Johnston
President and life member
of the Cooperative Growers Association
and the Jamaica Agricultural Society
farmer and shoemaker by trade
Church of England by religion.
I greet you as man to man.
Me teck you as me see you
and trust that you do the same,
for when you see me, me see you
when you no see me, me no see you
so chin-chin and good luck
hope we will be no more strangers.

Obeah Dung Deh

Old public works watchman Palanka
getting on in years can't do much
planted several cho-cho vines for his support
on his place near the roadside
making a good living from the green and white fruit
for when is reaping time
higglers come from near and wide
to buy them by the bushel basket full.

But soon thieves were upon him
picking all even the young and stainy
and there was none left for him to sell.
Resolving to catch the culprits
he waited up night after night
but without success for he soon fell asleep
and by the time he woke
they had come and gone
and now he was flat broke.

Soon he hit upon a plan
that would prey on their superstition.
In a clear glass bottle
he mixed up some ugly blue water
caulked it with an english cork
into which he stuck three of the biggest needles
he could find.
Attached to that he had a little threadbag of red cloth
filled with oil-nut seeds and three kinds of weeds,
three johncrow feathers tied with a piece of black string
long enough to tie it to the bottle
this he placed on a crude cross of cedar branches
and the whole contraption he stuck up near the vines
in clear and full view of all who passed by the road.
As he did so he chanted a strange sounding tune
the same one he sang sprinkling from a vial
whenever he took it down
so he could safely reap
making sure there were observers
to see this necessary ritual.

Would you believe that from the very first day
that he put up this thing
everybody thief and all
walk by in fear and trembling
and the word went round
obeah dung deh.
No one would venture near
not even to beg the usual pan of water
from his always full tank
absolutely sure some disaster would befall
whoever even looked too hard at the vine .
Now there is more than enough to sell
and Palanka is happy laughing all the way
to the Parish P.C. Bank.

School Days

Marbles

Inside the school yard
where the dirt is hard
boys crouch beside the circle
crudely drawn, faces set
shirt backs wet,
nichol and cashew seeds
jostle tough iron and pretty glass marbles
chinked from expert knuckles
to test the skills gain the thrills,
big boys and little boys alike,
bare knees sporting old bruises.
Rivals' pockets fill up empty in turn
a fight or two settle some games all in the fun.
Winners flaunt their victories
taunt the losers
as they slink home in the hot noon sun
promising next time, next time,
then the laughter and the rhyme
as champions write their names
in the bare loose dirt
with streams of warm amber ink.

Midnight Train

The darkness descends
after the evening showers
the air is full of cricket and toad songs
mating calls of night creatures
echo across the village
from bush and thicket.
No star appears
no moon penetrates
the dark lingering clouds
hanging curtains
hiding the night sky.
The darkness grows so thick
seems you can almost hold it,
not even a friendly firefly
winks at a passerby.
Then, a tiny light appears
piercing the darkness
growing with the sound
at first like far off thunder
of the midnight train
roaring down the tracks
slicing the pitch darkness
drowning every other sound.
For a moment only
the light touches the still wet grass.
Clinging raindrops
on leaves and stems
catch the swiftly passing light,
and a million gems sparkle.
Too soon it's gone
the lightgate closes
the split darkness joins once more
making it darker than before
and the night settles down
to wait for the welcome light of morning.

Fight

Fight! Fight!
The word echoes
across the class
in a flash
boys and girls
big and small
dash into the quiet yard.
The ring soon forms
on the grass around the bare patch.
Contenders groan,
vile threats resound
the boxing match
becomes a wrestling bout
as khaki pants, shirt and dirt blend,
become one.
Bodies roll each over the other
together all about
choking, cursing, clawing,
swearing, sweating.
From ringside watchers urge
and cheer their favourite,
would-be coaches hurl instructions
and directions from afar
"Lick him, kick him, tump out im granny,
box him, siddung pon him,
squeeze out him giznick."
Then somebody loudly whispers
the magic word
that ceases all strife
stops all war
T-E-A-C-H-E-R!
In a while
she walks across the broken circle
the fighters disappear
threatening tomorrow
hiding the pain.
Sweet cherub faces
with eyes of innocence
greet her knowing smile,
the yard is quiet again.

Garden Day

Friday day,
only half day school,
and gardening day.
Some parents hate the rules
upper division boys
must work the garden
learn about the soil
how to plant and care animals and crops
how to use farming tools.
Tempers boil because
"me send mi chile
to learn outa book
dutty him han
can't make him into man."
Some boys like to plant,
others like teaching, tailoring or mechanic,
like cricket, literature, music,
drawing, singing and arithmetic.
Few like experiment with science.
Make good sense you think.
Pity no one helps them to choose.
Just do as you're told
and no one is bold enough to differ
let alone refuse.
And the conflict between home and school
rocks you like a fool to and fro
and it is the country
you know that will lose.

Cool Sweetness

Some days
the river
send out silver spray invitation
and me and mi fren dem
strip off all we clothes naked
splash, swim,
hunt janga
match size
pop rudeness joke
laugh again
sometime till almost dark,
that time boy
you know life good.

The best time of all though
is when I alone
middle day sun hot
burning mi skin
as I walk through the cool cool water
up to mi special spot,
lie down naked on top the rock
feel the water drop
like ten thousand tiny electric shock

cooling mi skin and mi head.
The pool of mi mind clear, clear
I close mi eyes
inhale the air
the water wash clean clean
since before time –
nothing in the world sweet so
Nothing –
The water drip, drip
making love to every part of mi nakedness
non stop
till mi whole body
shiver with the cool sweetness.
I get into myself
deal with myself.
Dem time so
I want nothing, nothing
for on my special river rock
unto myself
I man is king.

Next to Godliness

Inside the gateway
of our neat little house
on the main road of our village
Grandmother towers
tamarind switch poised
commanding yet another routine
clean up campaign.

And me as usual
outside by the street quiet like a mouse
struggling with the half-a-rake
with too few teeth
to pull into one convenient pile
all the paper, leaves,
drinks cartons, cigarette boxes
and plastic juice bags
all the while pretending happiness,
continuously asking one question.
Why should I have to
rake up their mess?
Mind you,

this is all in my head
for the answer comes
from inside the yard,
as Gran always reading my mind.
"Even though is not you
throw dem there
is in front of your yard.
So you best clean it up
to take shame out your eye,
it not sanitary.
Cleanliness is next to Godliness,
an besides that, you save you behind."

I have to agree
specially since I want
to avoid a repeat
of day before yesterday's encounter
with the tamarind switch.

Dress To . . .

Is bad luck
or is fool you fool?
You crazy or what?
You must be eat mad puss brains.
Lawd man
you know how teacher cross,
di strap you see roll up on im desk
we all know is Busha old horse-bridle
the same one im use to teck ride Satan
and dat was no ordinary horse
an is four tamarind switch im cut last week.
You really idle
for you know dat
still an all you bruck fight
right beside the glass case
wid all teacher tings dem
dat im prize more dan im wife
an you no satisfy
you haffi bruck di glass tu
today of all days.
You must be forget that any day
teacher dress like is cricket match im gwine play
we must know to stay far from im
quiet as mus mus
for dat time im drop lick as you sey fey
an is the nearest one to im get di blow
you get beatin fi di slightest ting
sometime fi nutting at all
innocent an deserving alike
make no difference
you have no defence.
Me form sick dem time deh
an you see if mi mother force me
an me haffi come a school
me don't form fool me don't play nor fight
for is hell to pay
any day
teacher dress up in a full suit a white

Story Time

Story from Death Row

A leaking one-room shack was home
in a part of town,
where poverty and badness meet
and walk together hand on gun every day every night,
where garbage pile up for weeks
on a narrow filthy street,
where gunshot sounds more than reggae beat.

My mother worked
my granny prayed
my sister and I played
in innocence
our older brother
stayed away most times.
We never saw him but we
learned to say "Our Father".
Sometimes no food, no water, no money
no medicine except bush
when my granny got sick.

Soon childhood innocence fled
I got cut from a fight in my head
my sister got a belly at fourteen
my mother cursed
my granny prayed
my sister played with her baby
I like my brother
stayed away most times
and forgot "Our Father".

Then one day
a man came in a big car.
After a big meeting and a lot of big talk
he was good to us or so we thought,
he gave us food,
some used clothes and we had fun
because I was sixteen
he took me for a walk behind the house
gave me a gun, to make me a man, he said.

My brother said I was a man already
so that night he found me a woman
I later learned one of his own
and I didn't sleep that night.
She made me do things I had only heard about
my body shook violently
and exploded white and sticky.

We moved to a Government house
no leaks, three rooms, a palace
with a flush toilet and shower
electric lights and people's malice.
My mother worked,
my granny prayed,
my sister whored
my brother and I
followed the man in the big car
all over the island
to party meetings, conferences and other business
we were official.
We vowed to follow him till we died.

Time passed
my brother had five baby mothers
I only had three, but a trailer load of girls besides
plenty to drink and eat
much weed to smoke
crack cocaine, speed and coke
we were the biggest in the area
no one could stop us, we were kings.
My mother cursed
my granny prayed
my sister made more babies
my brother and I ran things.

The runnings was cool
everyone was silent when we talked
others hid when we walked
police wouldn't come near, we were like gods.
Then one day there was a raid
police and soldiers galore
gunshots flying wild

left my brother and three officers dead
me without my manhood
no gun, no status, nothing
except a bullet lodged in my spine
and a secured cell that leaks,
like the old room when I was a child,
back where it began
awaiting the decision
hang or not to hang.

Now, my mother weeps
my granny prays
my sister curses her children.
The man in the big car says
he didn't know me well
but he gave money to bury my brother
and a smalls for my granny and my mother
he says that was his only responsibility,
he says he is sympathetic,
he says he is being good
I say,
he too will die like my brother
one day, one day, if I get out
I'll settle the score with him then.

And my mother weeps
my granny prays
my sister curses her children
especially the nice little boy now ten
to whom the big man gave one hundred dollars
and a promise to make him a man.

A Sad Story

We loved each other
my friend and I
sharing everything since I could recall,
our bed, our money, our food
our clothes, all we had
not counting the cost between us
it was so good.
We were the envy of those around
and that was the cause of our pain.
Urged by the malice of less happy souls
I heard he said
he heard I said
and we both listened
to what they said
forgetting what we said
of what we meant one to the other.
Then came the awful silence
for we said nothing,
in fact vowing never to speak together again.
Now all we share is the loneliness
the grief, the anger, and the pain.
Pity we did not listen to ourselves
more pity we listened to others
greatest pity we lost each other
we who lived and loved
so like true brothers.

China Town Story

What you name?
Who your Papa?
Ah me know
me know your father long long time
me know him long before you born you know.
Your father house in Tung San near near to my own
and your grandfather have plenty land,
thousands of acre
yes man your grandfather land
stretch one mountain
to nedder mountain far far
big big land.
But when the war come Government take all your land
give to poor people
ahi God.

Your father smart man you know
have good education in China
he number one in whole province
big big brains,
all the village respect him
he the only one in the village
who go to University – Ahi yah.
He Gung Foo expert too
beat up alla somebody
everybody fraid him –
one time plenty robber attack the house
your father beat five man alone you know
chase them away him one, Ahi God
never see somebody so strong.

Yes man
me know your father long time –
He marry Jamaican woman no?
No Chiney woman
he marry Jamaican brown woman
your madda that? She short and fat.
And your big sister pretty pretty girl
pretty like cash money.

Ahi God
you growing so big – me know when you little baby
big man now – how hold you –
eighteen! Ahi yah
you can marry now
you reddy to marry now –
me find nice young girl fi you
get plenty grand son for you Papa.
Yes marry nice Chiney girl
better than Jamaican girl.
Dem like too much sport,
too much pretty dress
spen all your money
on gold and silver jewellery all a time.
Chiney girl work in shop
save your money care you children
take good care of husband
Ahi yah
yes man me know your father
you mother, your whole family
long long time, me know
me no forget
Ahi yah.
What you name again?

Love (Lost) Story

Her thinning hair
shows the colour
of the exquisite silver case
a love gift
at their passion's dawning
meant to store the trinkets
of their precious memories
treasures of their secret dreams
made and cherished then.
So distant in the past that seems
for now he loves another
the way of fickle men
their affection changing with the moon.
Too soon, all too soon love vanishes
the precious silver box
now the hiding place
for her loneliness and her sorrow.
How sad the door where no one knocks
sadder yet the love with no tomorrow.

Poor Aunt Margaret

Aunt Margaret maiden spinster lady
married well past forty in Bethlehem Church
in white dress, gloves and veiled hat,
her married sisters brothers too
swore her virgin still at that
made lewd jokes about what was possible
what was not.

Known to be feisty, it was said
she permitted no man till then
though many sought the prize
rich, poor, young, not so young
worthy and otherwise.

Of all her racially mixed up relatives
she came out lightest in colour
blue-green eyes, "good" long brown hair,
freckles galore dotted her fair face.
She took that quite seriously
she was making no apology
who didn't like it knew where to go
it was her gift, God made her so
He made her white.
She was a model of proper manners and conduct
like Caesar's wife above reproach
in the village she earned the name Busha Missis,
and in constant denial she played the part
in daytime and at night.

The man she married
veteran of World War One
dutifully asked her hand
of her aging father
who gave his glad consent
happy at last to get her off.
The courtship properly then proceeded
as might be so expected
for a lady of her standing
always before lamplight

in the little sitting hall
with straight backed chairs
each covered with antimacassa
set apart safely out of touching reach
which would never do at all
for a lady of such lofty quality.
On her wedding day
Aunt Margaret spinster lady
modest maiden
blushingly shed the expected tears of any decent bride
in her lace 'kerchief if you please
her veiled face and manners
belied her long years in loneliness spent.
His deep dark handsome honest face
smiled happily and openly at everyone
signalling his triumph and merriment to come.
She, poor lady, spent all her married life
till she went to her grave well past ninety
all her days now done
explaining he was not really black
his skin tone showed that colour
because he worked a lot in the sun.

Aunt B's Days

My Aunt B
had no time to idle
no time to waste
her time was occupied fully
day after day
week after week
year after year
in a set ordered way
no fuss, no haste
till near a hundred
her Lord called her home.

On Monday starting bright and early
she washed the clothes
first white then coloured and print
bone dried them in the warm morning sun
collected them in the old bamboo basket
tied out the two ewes and the ram
before her meal of left over roast beef gravy
nice dry yellow, afoo, or renta yam.

Tuesday saw her patching
mending the clean and the holey holey
a job that seemed unending work
some more patch than original cloth.
After that, gungo peas and bammy
or a dinner of boiled green bananas
and corned pork.

Wednesday the log fire glowed in her yard
roasting plantain, breadfruit and saltfish
heating the sad-irons she used
to give the shiney smoothness to khaki, old-iron blue
cotton, rayon, her husband's white dress-shirt
her nice blouse and skirt
plaid, floral, stripe, old and new.

On Thursday she tended her little garden
near the side of the old house

out of the children's play,
where she planted
gungo peas, corn, seasonings callaloo
and scotch bonnet pepper
for the compulsory stew peas
on this Ben Johnson's day.
Friday the house was cleaned
spic and span, top to bottom
cleaned to the glorious open-throated strains
of "When the roll is called up yonder"
till the whole place glowed,
reeking with the sweet smell of bees wax and elderberry.
You could see your face, part your hair
in the splendid shine of the old wooden floor.
Fish kind was what she ate then.
End of month
the furniture was changed around once again
east for west, north for south
and clean crocus mats placed at every door-mouth.

Saturday off to market
to buy and sell and talk and laugh
with friends from up the hill,
round the hill, cross the river, over the hill.
Plenty to tell, good, bad
plenty to hear, happy, sad
plenty to get
leggins, goose neck, chocho, pumpkin, coco
for the thick beef soup
and shop-flour for tight tight dumpling.
Sunday morning was the best
worship, prayers, praise
and please God a little rest.
The rough work-garb
replaced by Sunday-day clothes
of finer material sober colours and style.
Before first bell started ringing
the rice and peas finished cooking
she was in the accustomed bench
looking happy and content
with her friends singing
ancient and modern hymns

Sankey, Crusade and Psalms
giving thanks, giving praise.

This is the way Aunt B lived
day after day, week after week
month after month, year after year
that was her story
till near a hundred
when the Lord called her home to glory.

Nana's Chalk Pipe

(for Ernie Ranglin)

The steep path winds up the hill
up to St. Simon's, Anglican.
Framed by the spreading branches of a great guango tree
this little cut stone church proudly sits
with the wooden belfry off to one side.

Clumps of Khus-Khus grass edge the walkway
holding the clay earth together
keeping the neat track safe
to get the faithful up the hill.

Nana over ninety years ripe with a back slightly bent
walks up to church amazing us all,
every Sunday rain or shine
since she was small
without help she gets to the top
she has a stick now
but, we are sure it's the chalk pipe that does the trick,
the pipe she says is her best friend.

She starts the journey
with a good pipe-full
stuffed with strong tobacco of the jackass rope variety
lit with a match on Sundays
not a live fire-coal as on other days.

Puffing smoke like a war time
wood burning train engine
slowly and surely she makes her way up,
up to the church, nearer to God
where savouring the last puff feeling good
she carefully knocks out the gray ashes
from the white chalk pipe,
finds a secure spot
in the Khus-Khus root
to hide her precious friend.
Much as she loves her smoke
the pipe and tobacco

must not enter the house of the Lord
when she goes in to praise her God,
world without end.

But dear Nana, bless her soul
try as she might
she could never remember
where in the grass she hid the last pipe,
so it's a new one every week
January to December
you can imagine how many pipes
she's lost in the sweet smelling grass
after all one clump of Khus-Khus is like any other.
If you hear Nana
"Blessed Saviour pilot me, I can't find the blasted pipe,
the damn Khus-Khus so confusing,
and the price a pipe gone up again
to shilling and quattie
I woulda give anything to find even the
halfa-pipe."

We children waiting for that call
search and find them
sometimes two at a time or more
for the grateful old lady
generously hands out handsome rewards, and praise
"What would I do without you lovely children"
as if by magic
out of the bottomless depths of her bib pockets
comes coconut cake, candy bump,
asham, toe toe cake
whatever she decides to make that day,
or the day before.
So you know it's very often we children go
in search of Nana's precious white chalk pipe.

Man of the Morning

On a bright morning he was born
to his father and his lawful wife.
He sang on a bright morning
the happy songs of childhood life.

On a bright morning he wed
his lovely lady wife,
welcomed his first born son
into his early adult life.

He passed away on a bright morning,
No fuss, no tears, no strife.
On a bright morning we laid him down to rest
to his soldier music, trumpet, drum and fife.

Who Stronger

You ever see anything so
how some things get to be known as facts
just because some ignorant person
say it often enough
even when nothing no really go so
boy it really rough.
Some people see only what dem want to see
hear only what them want to hear,
so them come up with all kinds of stupidness
that everybody believe and take for gospel.

You take this man and woman business
you tired to hear say woman weaker than man
or that man stronger than woman, big argument.
Take it from me, no need fi no war
nothing no go so.
Me must know me grow up,
with mi mother, mi five sister and mi four aunty
and a three wife me married already.

Woman is stronger than man by far.
Maybe man can lift up heavier load yes
have more body strength
but put them to the tess
that is as far as it go.
Take mi uncle, suppose to be
a strong tough man six foot tall
full a mouth and big chat
when him wife dead, kiss mi neck
him bawl and bawl
bruck dung to nutten, lose all him fat
almost two years him teck
to come back to himself.

My aunt now, she lose her husband and daughter
in the same accident one day
it was a sad, sad thing
and see yah sah she ban her belly
and make the first bawling

rub her face with little white rum
read two psalms
and after she bury dem
it was business as usual.
Man weak yah, weak like rat.
You think anyone a we
could bear baby pain?
Talk the truth, who?
We woulda dead
for we can't stand a little fresh cold
or even a little flu.
We have to wrap up
scrunch up in the bed, tie up wi head
and call fi wife and girl friend
mother aunty and sister
or you ole granny.

If you don't want to get me vex
don't talk no foolishness
bout woman weaker than man.
Any body you hear say that
dem don't know a thing bout woman
nor anything at all bout sex.

"Interferance"

You ever see me trial
what crosses a set pon me dis day?
Massa God you see
how this woman provoking?
Come a try upset mi liver
when me and she don't have nothing what so ever.
Me don't talk to her more than so you know
except good how-di-do
Me and Parson have a little disagreement
and me and him argue it out
me let him know how me feel
after all me a flesh and blood like him
no mine say him have big position an power.
Now all of a sudden
dis oversize woman come a try buy out the argument
an want to reap up the old story again
as if to say she a Parson mouth piece.
Dem tings no call for
for me and Parson one settle wi business
like two responsible people
an the matter done.
Parson naw belch, but she a vomit

him head naw hurt him
but she a have heart attack.
Must be praise she a look
for she no stan fi get one farden.
Me did think dem days done
but it still a gwan
Backra cut fart
nayga ask pardon.

Argument

They were playmates and cousins a long time ago
he was younger, overgrown and precocious
she neat and petite a real little doll
with a razor sharp tongue
she saw him as a loving cousin brother and sister like
he spent many sleepless nights wanting her
his flesh rigid and burning,
so he tried in all manner of ways
with all his might to seduce his pretty shapely cousin
but she would have none of it for it was not right.

At age twenty one
she married a Westmoreland man and moved far away.
He took his broken heart over the far side of the island
where he went to work in St. Thomas as a farm hand.
Time passed they both married well
lived good prosperous and happy lives
matter of fact he married two wives
a second when the first one passed away.
Each had several children plenty grand
much property and prestige galore
as he grew more mature
he thought of her less
and what might have been
if he had had his way.
Now and then he crossed her mind
as with amusement
she told her children of their puppy love days
as he told his sons of his beautiful cousin
and how their lives went separate ways.

Strange in all this time they hadn't met again
until nearly fifty years later for a large reunion
at a moonlight hop on the big barbeque
where the family had gathered from near and far
to celebrate the marriage of one of their clan.
That night polka and quadrille raising cane
he found himself dancing with her face to face
as in their young days they took over the floor

for they were two of the best you could ever see
so the story of their skill was legend in the family
as was the story of his love she did not return.

To see these two old folks dance was a real treat
he still nimble and quick on his aging feet
she with waist still trim supple and strong
making movements to put the young to shame
still dancing their fame they had every one delighted
all other couples stopped dancing gave them the floor
now they and the musicians challenged one another
till dancers and musicians were hot in competition,
the crowd cheering shouting for more.

Meanwhile older folks called out to the young
to observe how the quadrille should really be done
to take good stock of properly dance polka
it was a long time since they had seen anyone dance
with such grace and style such elegance and enjoyment.
Finally energies spent musicians and dancers stopped
and the two oldsters flopped in each other's arms
laughing heartily at the thrill they had just known.
Josiah quite beside himself with excitement and joy
was the first to catch his breath enough to speak.

"Ellen gal ah you" he said trying to contain himself.
"Is me same one Josiah" she was cool as a cucumber.
"But you can still dance a good number" said he
"You not so bad yourself you don't forget how" said she
"Long time now we don't meet, nearly fifty year"
he breathlessly said
"Forty nine years four months and one week"
she quietly corrected
"You still looking good you know sweet chile"
he complimented
"You not looking bad yourself mister Josiah"
she openly flirted
"And you know how long I did want to make a thing wid you"
Right then everyone realised that argument begin
the circle tightened around the two fencing them in
Josiah misread what he took for a cue,
"Oh go away Josiah you are an old man,

make you age protect you" said she waving her fan
"You never hear say the older the violin the sweeter it play an
the older the moon the brighter it shine"
he said smiling.
"Well you not no moon, and every violin have to have a stiff
bow with plenty rasam to play at all much more sweet, you too
ole fi dem things deh."
Now getting a bit flustered
Josiah sensed she was winning
he had quite forgotten her sharp tongue ready wit
and body movement that always sent his head spinning
but he couldn't quit now
trying to recoup he gleefully said
"Ole? Go bout you businis, if anyone ole a you,
memba say when me was a little boy inna short trousis
you was a big young miss a breasted"
he was on the attack
but the old lady was just as quick with the come back
"So wat dat have to do with the price of prementa
you too outa order. Ole or no ole understan one thing
you couldn't exercise me in no way shape nor form
pon the level up the grade on the stretch or in the ring."
Poor Josiah instead of backing down gracefully
made one more try, his face flushed and warm
"You still full a chat eh Ellen Gal,"
he was getting a little mad
"Why you don't put your action whey you mouth deh
and take up the challenge if you think you bad."
What followed completely floored Josiah
for he had nothing more to say in this argument
Miss Ellen pulled herself to her full five foot four inches
as the crowd stood riveted to the spot
in perfect silence heard her deliver the parting shot
"Oh go away from me, shut you boasy chat
mouth make a thousand drawers
and backside don't wear one
so done the argument,
save you breath fi cool you tea cup
remember say all woman can lie dung
ah no all man can tan up."

We is the Best

No mam
I am not surprised
at all, at all
not surprised one bit
Miss Alice granson turn big Doctor
in a big hospital in 'Merica.

Matter of fact I did expect it
after all him grand father
was a head teacher for umpteen years
and him great granpa was elder in the church
and was the finest carpenter you could get
and the great uncle was the bessis coffee farmer
in the whole island.
Dat was just on the grand mother side.

When it come to the grand father side –
dem is another set of substantial people
come from over Portland.
Yes mam –
the great, great, great granpa was a Maroon warrior
cut English soldier backside,
up and down hill and valley.
The great great uncle
was overseer on the biggest property in the parish.
The great granpa was an ordained minister
and fi him brother study fi dentist.
One cousin is engineer whey build bridge.
Even though him second cousin is a shuffler
when it come to dis one now
mi no know how
you coulda surprise
say him reach so far
after 'Merica man no better dan him.
And even if him come from poor circumstances
member ugly cockroach cut pretty cloth.
Is through you no know the history
for if you check far back eena wi pedigree
back whey wi come from

some a wi fore parents
was people of Nobility, Royalty
offa good table
outa good stock –
some was Chief and King and people of worth
so no shock, no surprise when you see
one of wi own birth
come out to something grand.
We a somebody to, like anybody else
from any which where
we come from somewhere
we no drop from sky
a no old zinc and tinnin meck we –
we is the best.
Anything we put wi han to – the simplest one a wi
wi beat out all the rest.
A who you think is all di professional dem
in di country
is fi wi owna boys and girls
man and woman who spring from wi same one
fi wi owna generation, no importation.
And you no want no better example
than right here in the district –
Miss Alice gran son turn big Doctor
Aunt Bess daughter is head nurse
Miss Ellen step son is Insurance Executive
Miss Jess nephew is Custos
Miss Lyn one son is head Anglican Bishop
Missa Chin son a fly big Air Jamaica plane
an Missa Ramsing bwoy a big computer expert
Benji nephew is Permanent Secretary.
And Na Na Zella gran son
the one who unno give the nick name
bring fame and pride to wi all –
For look how the big head bwoy
tun big Governor General.